DATE DUE

MACHAQUILÁ

MACHAQUILÁ

Through the
Mayan Jungle
to a Lost City

by ALBERT LISI

HASTINGS HOUSE • PUBLISHERS   New York

To My Parents
John and Lena Lisi

Published simultaneously in Canada
by Saunders, of Toronto, Ltd.
Don Mills, Ontario

Library of Congress Catalog Card Number: 68–17649

Printed in the United States of America

CONTENTS

Contents   6

LIST OF ILLUSTRATIONS

(Following page 128)

Part One

The Long Drive

~~~~~~

1 · A DREAM . . . A PLAN . . . AN ACT

FOR YEARS I had thought about making a trip to the jungles of Guatemala but commitments kept me from taking the final plunge. Now I was determined to go and I laid out my plan. I knew it would take a sizable amount of cash. While I saved I would find out all I could about the area I had decided to go to. I had to check out equipment and choose the best, what I needed and what I would not need. Lastly, I determined my transportation; I would drive down rather than fly.

In anticipation of my coming adventure, I began to research. I haunted the library, reading book after book by previous travelers in the Mayan area and texts on the ancient Mayan empire. This greatest of all pre-Columbian civilizations covered Guatemala, British Honduras, the Mexican states of Yucatan, Campeche, Quintanaroo territory, most of Chiapas and Tobasco and parts of Honduras and El Salvador;

an area roughly the size of California, and larger than either the British Isles or Germany. The more I read the more my imagination grew. Almost every year a *chiclero*—a gatherer of chicle, used in making chewing gum—would discover some new ruin or mound in the jungles. It is estimated that there are two hundred still undiscovered ruin sites in the Mayan area. My imagination flamed, and I too dreamed of finding a new ruin in these same jungles.

I needed a map with all the known ruins marked on it. But what a problem—no such map existed! I checked a dozen. Each had fifty or sixty ruins marked on it, but most were duplicates of what the other maps had. Finally I had an idea. If each map had a few new ruins listed, all I had to do was get enough maps, combine them, and make my own. It was a demanding project, but I decided to tackle it and pored over hundreds of maps.

Finally, after a year of finding and checking new maps, I completed mine. It had almost 250 ruins marked on it. As the map took shape, so did an idea. The completed map confirmed my hopes. If there are at least 200 still undiscovered ruins in this area—and I had more than that number listed on my map—then what was in the blank spots on the map? More ruins, of course. I was amazed and elated. There may be another map like it, or even better, but if so no one is showing it.

My interest lay in the deep rain-forested jungles of El Peten, the northern jungle state of Guatemala. Ten thousand square miles, remote and in parts virtually inaccessible, El Peten still guarded its unknown ruins. My map showed two likely areas in the Peten, where no ruins were marked.

All Mayan ruins are built on or near water, a primary requisite for any city. They are on rivers, near lakes or *cenotes*. A *cenote* is a cave-in of surface limestone, forming a huge well. As these occur only in the north of the Yucatan Peninsula, they do not need to be considered in the Peten. This leaves rivers and *lagunas*. As *lagunas* of any size have known ruins near them, only the rivers were left.

The two areas I chose were ideal. Both had rivers ribbing their entire sections. The northern one centered around the Rio San Pedro. The southern one was traversed with streams running into the Rio De La Pasion, the largest river in El Peten. I had a choice. Both areas have jungle airports, of which there are eight in the Peten. The one on the San Pedro was called Paso Caballos (Pass of the Horses—Cortez marched through it on his conquest). The southern area, off the Pasion, had an airport at Poptún. I decided to try the area around Poptún first.

In the spring of 1964 my mind was made up. I was ready to leave. All I needed was money. I figured a thousand dollars would do it. I obtained a passport and straightened out my affairs. Then in September I sold five paintings. I bought a 1955 Rambler station wagon, my carefully chosen jungle equipment, which included a two-man rubber boat, outboard motor and rig, and I was ready to go. After I had put the car in tip-top repair and paid for all the equipment, I was left with only $300. I had figured I would need a minimum of $600 for the trip, when I was ready to leave. Should I try for the additional $300, and chance losing it in the rat race of New York City, or go short?

It was now or never, and I knew it. So on October 18, 1964 I drove out of New York City and began the long drive.

What makes a man climb a mountain, sail an ocean, explore a jungle—or build a financial empire, for that matter? Many people had asked me: Why was I going into the Guatemalan jungle?

The answer was simple. I was following a dream, a dream of discovery. I had a compelling, almost unconscious desire to rediscover the past, and in it mankind and myself. A mystic might imagine that I had once lived, as a Mayan, a previous life in that long lost empire in the Central American jungle. I had no such illusion, but the speculation does titillate the imagination.

Throughout history, some men's dreams have been so vivid that they experienced them as visions. They were not real, only extraordinarily daydreams, sharp and clear and convincing. Some of these men may have been mad; many later on were made saints. What actually happened was that they simply never woke up. But the why of the dream—why a man wants to search after it, to discover or to conquer—is another question.

The realist gives an obvious answer: Man's natural curiosity ("because it is there"); man has an inborn desire to keep busy, to keep his mind occupied. This may be true—but why explore or conquer? Most men are content to sit in an office all day, doing work that really does not interest them, or to operate a machine whose final product has no particular value to them. There are sheep and goats in the world; there are followers and leaders. All dream but few act: it is easier to do nothing.

Among the leaders have been the explorers, the great military commanders, scientists like Galileo, artists like Gaugin. Their personalities have been varied but basically they all have been explorers.

Of course the explorer-adventurer actually takes off along the unbeaten trail and searches for the strange tribe, the lost city. The archeologist lays claim to being both explorer and scientist but in the final analysis he is truly the latter: he is more interested in digging, classifying and deciphering than in the actual finding. He is a patient man, more at home in the laboratory than in the field. The explorer is a man of action—on the slightest clue to or unconfirmed story about some faroff lost city he may let his imagination take over for awhile and then is ready to strike out. New worlds to conquer—or, rather, old worlds. Providing, of course, that he can scrape up the necessary funds.

I should state at this point that I am an artist—a painter. Obviously art is not enough exploration in my case, although it is my chosen profession. It has been so with many explorers. Heinrich Schliemann, who took Homer literally and discovered and excavated Troy in the 1870s, was neither explorer nor archeologist, but a millionaire banker, whose main hobby was languages (he spoke thirteen fluently). John Lloyd Stevens, an American lawyer and diplomat, explored the Mayan area in the 1830s and '40s, as did Count Jean Frederic Waldeck, a German artist and soldier of fortune.

Two of the great decipherings of ancient languages were not done by archeologists at all. In 1802 a German teacher, George F. Grotefend, unraveled the mystery of cuneiform writing. He was only twenty-seven at the time, and did it in two weeks to win a bet. Scholars struggled with Cretan script for fifty years, until in 1953 a young English architect, Michael Ventris, accomplished the feat. Someday the still undeciphered Etruscan writing may fall to an amateur. Could it be that imagination is more valid than education, or is it just that education sometimes lacks imagination? In any case, those who look for unconscious motivations, like Freudian enthusiasts, might be interested in the following aspect of my childhood.

Several times each year, from the time I was five until I was ten or eleven, my parents would take me to the Museum of Natural History in New York City. I came to know and love all the rooms and exhibits, but none fascinated me as much as the dioramas of jungle scenes. We also visited the Metropolitan Museum of Art, across Central Park. I always loved the paintings, but was constantly fascinated by the models of ancient temples. In these two museums there was only one room which combined jungle and ancient temple in one setting—the Central American Room of the Museum of Natural History (since remodeled, 1965–68).

As I grew older, the pull toward art and painting took precedence in my dreams of creating, but my dream of someday exploring the jungle for ruins remained with me. For exploration, whether in art or in the act of exploring itself, is always creating.

There are two basic forces in man: creation and destruction. Explorers fall into both categories but are overbalanced on the creation side. The military man, although he explores, destroys. The artist, scientist, builder of industrial empires and the explorer on the trail create. First comes the dream, then a plan, and finally the act.

I drove day and night on the turnpikes, averaging sixteen hours a day and pulling off for sleep whenever I became tired. The car was old so I never pushed it much over fifty miles an hour. Hundreds of cars passed me daily. But one by one, the states fell behind . . . New Jersey, Pennsylvania, Ohio. Across northern Indiana with its unique flat expanse of midwestern autumn: nostalgic Americana. My unknown, ever-distant destination pulled me like a magnet. I crossed over into Illinois and headed for St. Louis, where I arrived on the third day.

In St. Louis I stayed with some friends, Ken and Franca Tielkemeier, and their little daughter Inghe. Ken and Franca are both artists. They had recently returned from Italy and had some two hundred paintings to show me. Ken's work had changed, and he had some great new things which we discussed at length. I hadn't seen them for three years, and what with the paintings, the relaxed atmosphere of old friends and the talk of my proposed jungle trip, two days passed. I decided to stay for the weekend. On the fourth day the jungle fever was flaming again. I checked all my gear, rearranged and repacked everything, and was ready to go. I said good-by to the Tielke-meiers and headed south. Oklahoma was flat, period.

My first car trouble developed outside of Dallas. I lost a half day getting a new voltage regulator. When I arrived at San Antonio it was late at night. I stayed overnight in a motel so I could see the Alamo the next day. I was becoming more relaxed about the trip and found the Alamo interesting, but I have never made a good tourist. In four trips to Mexico I still haven't seen a bull fight.

Ten days after leaving New York, I reached the border at Laredo. I changed fifty dollars into 600 pesos and drove down to the bridge over the Rio Grande. The customs officials made a big thing out of me. The car was loaded with all sorts of goodies and they wanted to see everything. But I know these officials. Nice guys, if you give them a break. I let them get half way through my stuff and then handed out a few dollar bills. I had nothing to hide, but I was tired and not in the mood to hang around. Five minutes later I was over the bridge and into Mexico. Darkness had fallen.

2 · SOUTH OF THE BORDER

The Mexican road was a sharp contrast to our American highways. Narrower, unlit and lonely, it was nevertheless enchanting. I was alone on the road, bouncing along through a sea of darkness. After an hour, only two cars had passed me heading toward Texas. Then I saw a light up ahead. There was a small cantina on my side of the road. An old gas pump stood in front of it. I pulled off and stopped. The cantina was a small adobe block. The only light around was a dim one coming through the open doorway. I had stopped near a water faucet on the end of a pipe in the ground. I put some water in the radiator and then decided to go inside, as no one had come out. I wanted to try out my Spanish.

Inside there was a long wooden counter with a few boxes nailed to the wall behind, holding cigarettes, bottles of tequila and odds and ends. There was a pile of old newspapers in a corner, and on one wall hung a huge girlie calendar next to a broken mirror. The third wall had a door, covered over with a huge dirty blanket. But no one was around. *"Buenos noches,"* I called out. A minute later an old Mexican man came out from behind the dirty blanket, rubbing his eyes. The conversation began. He said he had been sleeping, asked if I were American, as if he didn't know, and maybe I wanted a drink? No? I said *si* and had a tequila. He said his name was Jose and told me the town was called Vallecillo. We chatted for a half hour.

I only mention this little episode because I really liked that old man. When I was ready to leave he wouldn't even let me pay for the tequila, of which on his insistance I had had two. I gave him a pack of Chesterfields as a gift. He gave me a pack of Mexican Casinos in return. We each opened our packs. I offered and he offered. I ended up with a Chesterfield and he with a Casino. Looking at each other we laughed, exchanged cigarettes and had another tequila. That's Mexico, when it's nice. He asked for my name on a piece of paper, so I had him sign my road map. Slowly and with great elegance, he spelled out Jose Ramirez. Before leaving, I had another tequila, which I insisted on paying for, and then said good-by.

I drove on through the black night, the radio now picking up several Mexican stations. At one in the morning I reached Monterrey, a fair-sized city, and although I wasn't impressed by its looks I liked it anyway. I drove through slowly, looking for a deserted street to park in. Coming to an archway in the middle of a large street, I drove around it and a short distance beyond pulled over to the curb. I jumped into the back and on my air mattress, between outboard motor and jungle paraphernalia, slept my first night in Mexico.

I woke up at six A.M. and headed out of town. The road wound up a hill and before I knew it I was lost. I asked directions from some laborers, just starting work by the side of the road, and was off again. The road out of Monterrey led south past high mountains to the left. I drove along beside them for an hour and then began to climb. Soon I was in a twisting pass, across the foothills of the mountains.

As the road began to descend, I noticed a strangeness in the feel of the wheel. Then on one curve to the left it refused to respond. I panicked for a second, but suddenly it caught and I swung to the center of the lane again.

Later the pass opened out and came level on a huge flat plain. Two minutes later I heard a sharp noise at the front of the car. I dragged to a stop by the side of the road. Damn, I thought, a flat! No such luck. Getting out of the car, I saw that the left front wheel was way up under the fender and bent out. It was no flat. The steering mechanism had let go.

I lit a cigarette and a strange feeling of hopelessness came over me. I looked around. I was who knows how far from anywhere. The flat expanse around me looked like no man's land. I started to work and jacked up the car. After an hour on that dusty road, under that greasy front end, I could see that I just didn't have the tools. What I really needed was another jack.

Awhile later a Mexican truck pulled up down the road behind me. The driver got out, lifted the hood and started to fuss with the radiator. I went up to him and asked him what the trouble was. He said the radiator was losing water and he didn't have any more left. I told him I'd give him five gallons if he would take me to the nearest town. It was agreed. Ten miles later, we pulled into Ramos Arizpe, an undistinguished wide spot in the road, but it had a mechanic.

I found him, and hitching a ride back from a passing car, we arrived at my sad-looking heap. After an hour of struggling with the thing, we got it back in place. What had happened was this: in place of a king pin, the steering had a large screw that fit into a threaded pot. This thread had stripped and slipped out. The mechanic told me to take it easy as we drove off. I asked if I could make it to Saltillo, fifteen miles away. He said *"Quizas si, quizas no"*—Maybe! I decided to try it. When he presented the bill, one hundred pesos, I was angry. I argued, but in the end I had to pay. I left town in a huff, hoping to make Saltillo before the steering let loose again.

Bumps were now an ever present danger, and there are no bumpier roads than in Mexico. I reached Saltillo an hour later. I decided to throw caution aside and headed out of town intending to make San Luis Potosi, 300 miles to the south. I would get the front end fixed there. I drove all afternoon through mountain country, passing through Matahula at sundown, and all night, going at a slow speed and trying to miss all bumps. Every now and then, however, I would bounce across one in the dark. I'd stop and check the position of the large screw with my flashlight. It had a two-inch leeway before it would slip out of the pot again. As long as it stayed no more than an inch out, I was safe. Uncertainly, I pulled into the cobble-stoned streets of San Luis Potosi, just before midnight.

3 · THE GANG AT SAN LUIS

SLOWLY, IN LOW gear, I threaded my way over the bumpy stones, until I saw what I was looking for. A *comida* (a sort of open kitchen-type restaurant). I was tired and hungry. I went in and asked what they had to eat. There was a señora of thirty and a boy and girl both in their teens. The señora said *tortillas* and *frijoles*, and I said *bien*, tortillas and beans.

The place was old and filthy, and had that cooking-grease smell, so common in popular Mexican *comidas*. There was an open-hearth affair with a fire going in it against one wall, and a doorway next to it, leading I couldn't tell where. The light was bad. The room only had a few tables and chairs and, what was undoubtedly the prize possession, an old twenty-record Wurlitzer jukebox. (Remember them?) I asked for the toilet, and was led through the doorway next to the hearth. The place was broken down and smelly. No light, water, sink or soap. Just a bowl in a cubicle.

Returning, my tortillas and beans were ready. I looked out and checked my car, which was across the street, and ate. I played a song on the juke box, to everyone's delight, paid the señora, said buenos noches, and left. It was a lonely part of town and the streets were empty. Back at the car, I crawled into the back and went to sleep.

I was awakened by a loud crash on the roof. Bolting up out of a dead sleep, I saw a boy run around a nearby corner. Otherwise the streets were deserted. I checked my watch. It was after two in the morning. I had slept only a few hours but I knew it was time to leave. I knew that any small boy up at this hour of the night was probably part of a Mexican kid gang. They have a habit of sending the youngest out first, to catch people off guard. Outwardly they are friendly and smiling, but they are dirt-poor and completely wild. A tough, dangerous breed.

I slipped into the front seat, but had trouble finding the key in my pocket. Before I could start the car, several boys trotted out from the corner and stood in front of it.

There were seven or eight of them and they seemed to be thirteen or fourteen years old. The oldest was at least seventeen and there was no doubt he was the leader. He made a few motions with his arms and they began drifting around the car. I was surrounded. Then he came up to the driver's side and tapped on my window. I cracked it four or five inches and asked what he wanted.

Nothing, he said smiling, just to talk. I looked around. Everybody was smiling except me. They could see I had the car loaded with things. To them even the old car was a treasure. They must have thought it a great stroke of luck. Here I was, a gringo, but obviously no ordinary tourist. In old clothes, in an old car, and sleeping in it, no less. Who would miss me?

The doors were locked, but I knew if I started the motor they would jump on the car and try to stop it. Besides, I couldn't speed away on that bumpy cobblestone street. The front end was sure to give way. As for fighting it out, that was madness. I had no pistol and my machete and knives were in my packs in the back. Already they were banging on the windows and the roof with stones, and I was sure there were at least four or five knives among them. I had one chance, my only one.

I kept talking to the leader and told him to stop them from banging. He laughed and said he couldn't. He asked where I was going. Mexico City, I said. He wanted a ride there. I said I didn't have room for all of them. He said No, no. Only he would come. If I would open the door, he said, he would really appreciate a ride to Mexico City. He would be quiet and ask for nothing.

No, I thought, only my goods and maybe my life. Making up a story, I said I couldn't take him. He was angry. It was against Mexican law, I insisted, for Americans to give rides to Mexicans. He became angrier and cursed, pulling a knife. I started the car and began moving in low gear.

The leader screamed furiously, cursing as I closed the window. One kid jumped on the hood and started to bang with his fists on the windshield. Luckily he was not using stones, but I heard one bounce off the side of the car. The leader and another boy jabbed at the windows with knives, then tried the tires. I was thinking about that bolt in the front end jumping out. If it did now, I thought, I was as good as dead. The car was taking a beating and now my fear had turned to anger. If I stopped, pulled out my machete and fought them, I'd only end up getting stoned or stabbed to death. I decided to take a chance on the front end.

I shifted into second, but kept it down to twenty miles an hour. They chased me for two blocks, bouncing rocks off the roof as I drove off. I was cursing them and praying for the front end, both at the same time. In five minutes I was out of town and back on the highway.

Well, I thought, that's Mexico—when it's bad.

4 · BREAKDOWN AND BANDITS

THE GANG AT San Luis had started the adrenalin flowing in me, and I wasn't at all sleepy. I turned on the radio and drove slowly all night. Before daybreak I pulled over to the left, across from the intersection leading to San Miguel Allende. There's an artists' colony there, but with my front end as it was, I didn't want to chance the extra eighty-mile round trip, so I went to sleep for a few hours. Waking up in daylight, I drove to a gas station that had a restaurant and ate breakfast.

By eight I had reached Queretaro and drove right through, figuring to make Mexico City by noon. Just before the toll road I was stopped at a customs check point. Every now and then they spring one on you in Mexico. Keeps you on your toes.

The toll road was no better than the other roads; in fact, it was worse. It had almost continuous washboard sections in it, and the car began shimmying at thirty-five miles an hour. I had to creep along at thirty, creating a traffic bottleneck, as it was all hills and curves.

On one particular downgrade, a huge first-class Mexican bus kept honking his horn, but I was over as far as I could get. Without warning he swept by me, almost sideswiping me off the road. I cursed him and his exhaust fumes as he cut me off. There were no shoulders on the road and I kept wondering what would happen if the front end let go.

At ten-thirty I was driving up a long hill curving to the left. I had just passed the sixty-six-kilometer marker, and was estimating I'd be in Mexico City by one P.M., when there was a terrible crash. For a few seconds I lost control of the car and headed into the left lane toward the on coming traffic. Just in time I managed to swing it over to the right side and dragged and bumped to a stop. Luckily I was off the pavement, as the curve had a seven-foot flat dirt shoulder. If I had been going a little faster, I would have crashed head-on into the passing cars.

I struggled for an hour with the jack, blocks and wrenches. But it was worse than the first time. I cursed my lack of luck. Another seventy kilometers and I would have reached Ralph, I thought.

My friend Rafael Ávila was a Veracruzano whom I had met in Mexico City in 1955. He had lived in California in the twenties, and spoke good English; now, after having run his own printing shop in Mexico City for many years, he had closed it and was manager of a larger one in another part of town.

I started to hitchhike. From previous experience, I knew most Americans would not pick me up. I tried to hitch a ride once years ago in western Mexico, twenty miles outside of

Guaymas. It was late at night and in three hours only ten cars, all Americans, passed. No ride. Then a Mexican truck driver gave me a lift.

It happened again. After a half hour and a hundred cars, a Mexican truck stopped. I had the car locked, so I jumped right in. He was what is considered a typical heavy truck driver. A giant of a man, he didn't say five words the whole trip. There was a stack of Mexican comics on the seat and he had Mexican rock and roll on the radio. He also chain-smoked, filling the cab with cigarette fumes. With the heavy load we crept along, constantly shifting and never going over twenty miles an hour except downhill. In this unlikely atmosphere of anxiety, smoke and raucous music, I once more entered the once proud empire of the Aztecs, Mexico City.

We drove through miles of broken-down suburbs and city outskirts, until finally he dropped me off at a good spot for a taxi. He was right. I thanked him, got out, and in two minutes I had a taxi.

I found Ralph at the new print shop and he was the same smiling, helpful gentleman as ever. I explained my situation and heard the bad news. The days of the dead had started, a Mexican holiday in which the dead are honored. It was now four o'clock Friday evening. Ralph told me there would be no mechanics to go out and fix my car until the following Wednesday. I said if I could get a set of wrenches, and another jack, I would do it myself. Ralph insisted I wait. He made several calls. Everyone had taken off already for the vacation, but I didn't dare leave that car loaded with equipment on the road alone overnight.

Finally at eight o'clock in the evening, I made a deal with a cab driver. The price for the ride out and help in fixing the car was a hundred pesos. He had a jack and set of wrenches, but said he had to stop by his brother's house first. We drove an hour to the opposite end of town and he went in the house for a few minutes. Then he came out. We drove back out onto the toll road, reaching my old wreck an hour before midnight. It was locked and still safe.

The cab driver told me I was lucky, as there were bandits out in the hills around that road. I told him he was kidding. No, he said, pulling a large .45-caliber pistol out of his jacket. He said he had borrowed it from his brother. I found it hard to believe, but not for long.

Almost no cars passed on the road as we worked. With two lanterns, two jacks, wrenches, blocks of wood and lots of elbow grease, we finally jumped the bolt back into the pot. It took two hours. I pulled out a length of quarter-inch nylon rope I'd cut for the occasion and together we tied the mechanism so the bolt couldn't come out again. If I'd thought of it the first time, I'd have saved the whole thing from happening again.

Just as we were getting things straightened out and I had paid the cab driver, I thought I saw someone on the embankment above us. I threw the spotlight of one lantern over there. Two men were kneeling down not fifty feet away. At first they looked like farmers, with sombreros and the typical white outfits on. One was holding a machete and the other had a rifle folded in his arms.

"*Bandidos!*" the cabbie yelled, and grabbed the lantern out of my hands, turning it off.

We both dropped behind my car as a shot rang out and ricocheted off the road behind us. The cab driver pulled out his .45, crouched behind a fender, and let two rapid shots fly in the direction of the bandits. There was no reply. Then he told me to get into my car quietly, gave me a plan and said goodby. The plan was this: he would go to his car and wait. When I started my motor, if there were any shots he would fire twice again and then start his car and leave. This would give us both a good chance to escape. We figured they only had one rifle and that it was probably a single-shot.

I waited until I was certain the cabbie was in his car, then started my motor. There was no sound from the bandits. I heard the taxi start up and still no sound. We started slowly up the hill. After a hundred yards I saw the taxi's lights go on, so I switched mine on too. Then another single shot rang out. It wasn't a .45, it was a rifle. We sped off down the road and stopped after a few miles. I asked the cabbie if his car had taken a hit. He said he thought so. Sure enough, there was a hole in the right front fender, just missing the tire, but it was only a twenty-two rifle hole. Again I thanked the cabbie for his help.

"What if we hadn't finished fixing the car when they arrived?" I asked him.

"What if I hadn't had this?" he smiled, patting the pistol in his belt.

It was another close call, I thought. Again I said good-by to the cabbie, and he drove off in a rush. Slowly I started out for the city, and at four in the morning, arrived at the Paseo De La Reforma. All lighted up, silent, with no traffic or people, it was a strange and majestic sight. After an hour I found a reasonable hotel, where I could put the car inside, took a shower and, exhausted, went to bed.

The next day I met Ralph at the shop. I insisted on getting a pistol. I didn't mention the bandits for fear the cabbie had killed one. He had told me not to say anything about the incident to anyone. Ralph said I didn't need a pistol. I maintained I needed one for my jungle trip. Ralph, for some reason, told me you couldn't buy one in the gun shops any more. I guess he thought I'd get into trouble with one and besides he didn't really believe I was actually going into the jungle anyway. I told him I was definitely going, and began to search for a used pistol and the mechanic on my own. I found neither. On the fifth day I went downtown, walked into an *armería* and walked out with a new pistol. It was expensive but worth it. I said nothing to Ralph; I could see his point. Abandoning the idea of getting the car fixed, I said good-by to Ralph at eight that evening, thanked him for all his help, and drove off in a driving rain toward Puebla.

·On the Mexican plateau, this was supposed to be the dry season, but then the weather is always surprising one in the tropics—as is everything else.

5 · STRANDED AGAIN

SOMEHOW I GOT on the wrong highway outside of Mexico City, and couldn't get off. An hour passed before I found a gap in the road divider and went back. After some hours the rain stopped and I pulled into a gas station some seven kilometers outside of Puebla. There I met a young cab driver from town named Paco, who was in trouble. Remembering my own recent ones, I knew how he felt. He needed a push home. I had a coffee and then pushed him all the way to his house in Puebla.

There Paco brought out his guitar and some tequila, and we had a little fiesta. His wife, bleary-eyed and out of bed, didn't seem to mind, but smiled, listened and finally served us coffee. This at four in the morning. She hardly spoke. Finally he told me she was sick and I offered some aspirin which she gladly accepted. On top of it, she had a cold and had never complained. Only in Mexico, I thought. Or, I should say, never in the U.S.A.

I went to sleep in the car and woke up at nine the next

morning. I had breakfast with Paco, his wife, who was feeling better, and their two small daughters. At ten I said adios and drove off, on the road to Oaxaca.

Ten miles out of Puebla and about ten miles from the road, rises the majestic 17,893-foot cone of Popocatépetl. Although Pico De Orizaba, ninety miles dead east, is 427 feet higher, and the tallest mountain in Mexico, Popo is still the most beautiful. Clouds were drifting around the peak, the day was clear, and it was a perfect view across the fields. I stopped and took a photograph.

All day I drove through barren but beautiful mountain country, the road twisting around 180-degree turns, with a rolling 500-foot drop on the left, and always a spectacular view waiting around the next curve in the road. Keeping my speed under forty, I braked and rattled around tight, washboard curves, some banked as much as thirty degrees. I've never liked roller coasters, but this giant of a roller-coasting road was a thrill; challenging and beautiful.

I drove all day and night and into the next morning, getting a few hours' sleep, and then I was off again on the highroad. At sunrise I was descending into a valley, and at nine o'clock I rolled right into the center of Oaxaca, parking next to the *zocalo*, the central park-square. After a quick breakfast, I started out of town and soon reached the road climbing up to Monte Alban, the Zapotec ruin.

Although it was paved, it was barely fifteen feet wide. It wound like a series of snaking S's attached to the mountain, which towered solid rock on the left and became an increasingly higher drop on the right. I could see the thin line of the road up ahead on the mountain, that would appear to be the final curve left. Later, when I was approaching this curve, I looked to the right for a second, and saw a sheer thousand-foot drop to the valley below. I turned my eyes back to the road and a split-second later saw a horrifying sight. A truck shot around the curve only fifty feet ahead and seemed to take up the whole road. I hit the brake with a stomp, swerved to the edge of the cliff, and the truck dashed by on the left, finally blowing his horn as he passed. How he missed me I'll never know, but one thing is sure. Between the roads and the drivers, there's never a dull moment while driving through Mexico.

Finally the road became so steep I started to stall on one particular curve. I was in second. I tried to get it into low, but stalled. I put the emergency brake on but it wouldn't hold. I tried to start the car but couldn't, because I had to hold my foot on the foot brake. I was sliding back now, on this forty-five degree incline, on a cliff and around a curve. I almost panicked but got a hold of myself. With the hand and foot brakes I rolled back slowly and reached a fairly level spot. Now the hand brake held. I looked at the cliff and valley below. Not this time, I said to it silently. I started the car, put it in low, and barely made it to the level plateau above. I parked, and there was a magnificent view of Oaxaca below. Then I went into the ruins.

The ruins are not overly large. The main temple pyramid is across a 200-yard plaza with smaller structures on either side. I walked over to it and climbed to the top. It was fully restored and rebuilt, but although interesting it was not my cup of tea. That was why I was going to the jungles. Not only to see ruins in the jungle, which was my real aim, but to see ruins untouched and unrestored by man. Better a crumbling, untouched ruin than a reordered restored one. I can't say I was disappointed, though. I had expected this tourist attraction to be restored. What surprised me, however, was the cement between every stone holding it all together. I thought that was overdoing it.

I drove down that suicide trail of a road, this time with more of an idea of its dangers, and headed right out of town. I was looking for a ruin that had been discovered only a few years before and promised to be more to my taste.

About ten miles out of town, I noticed a small sign on the right but passed it. Backing up, I found that I had reached the ruin. A small sign read *Yagul*; no arrow, nothing. I guessed it must be up the dirt road on the left side of the highway. Starting up it, the dirt soon became a mass of sharp stones. I could see a shack way up ahead. Finding I couldn't make the incline in that sliding sand and rock, I left the car and walked it. Reaching the shack, I found a man and a boy inside.

"Yagul?" I asked. "*Si*," the man said. I followed them up another hill and into the ruin.

It was composed of a labyrinth of walls. There was a small main plaza and many small roomlike enclosures. No doubt at one time these smaller areas had been roofed, and it appeared certain that Yagul had been more of a residential area than a ceremonial center. My self-appointed guide showed me everywhere, and now and then I would find a potsherd in the dust. I must have picked up at least fifteen of them. I took a few pictures and after giving my guide some pesos, I left.

It was almost sundown by the time I reached the highway, so I decided not to stop off at Mitla, the famous ruin down the road. It was only another version of Monte Alban as far as I was concerned. Restored and full of tourists.

I drove into the setting sun, the sky orange and crimson, and kept going past Mitla. Soon I was out of the valley again and in the mountains. After awhile I noticed that the lights were going dim. I kept driving, hoping to make some village before they went dead. But there was nothing around. After an hour they went out completely. I had to stop. There I was, in the blackest night and most deserted place I had yet seen in Mexico. Huge trees overhung the roadway. I had not seen one car in the last two hours! It was no place to stop and sleep overnight. A town was marked on the map and I estimated I couldn't be more than five or ten kilometers away from it. I took out my spotlight battery lantern and tied it to the side-view mirror. Adjusting it to shine ahead, I started out in low.

In this fashion I crept along for a mile or so. Then the motor stopped. I couldn't start it. Luckily I was at the edge of a downgrade. I managed to push the car to it and rolled another half kilometer to the bottom of the hill. But there I stayed.

After a half hour I heard a motor in the distance, behind me. Then I saw a light. I waved it down. It was another Mexican truck, filled with workmen. They were all shouting and talking and appeared drunk, but they said they'd give me a push to Totalápan. How far? Only down a few more hills, they said. They started pushing me and away we went. A few kilometers later, we rolled into Totalápan, and the truck kept going.

I stopped in front of the only building I saw, a long wooden structure. There were only a few families, living in and running a sort of *comida* in this one building, and as I later found out this *was* Totalápan.

I had something to eat and later a car of the Mexican Tourist Patrol stopped, with two men in it. It was the first I'd seen or heard of. After looking over my car they decided, with some dispute, that I had a short in my light system. I could have told them that, but I thanked them for their help anyway. They left and I went to bed in the back of the car.

The next morning, I washed up and ate at Totalápan and soon got a push out of town. The motor started and I was O.K. I didn't need lights, and as long as I didn't stall I might make it to Tehuantepec, about a hundred miles away. By midmorning the car was bucking badly. I continued at twenty miles per hour, but it was getting worse. Finally at the next town, I had to stop. I had reached El Camarón.

I checked the car. I suspected the fuel pump or the generator, or both. An hour later the Mexican patrol stopped again. This time they decided that the armature of the generator had burned out and the car was running on the battery alone.

They pushed me ten kilometers up a long grade, but soon I was bucking badly and had to stop. I started to roll back to El Camarón and the patrol left. They had advised me to take the generator off and get it rewound. There would be a bus coming through for Tehuantepec today, but the schedule was unsure. Back in El Camarón, I started to remove the generator. But I didn't have time. At two P.M. the Tehuantepec bus arrived and I had to jump on.

I sat behind the driver and asked how far Tehuantepec was. The driver said it was 125 kilometers (seventy-five miles) to town. I sat back and tried to relax. The bus was second class. That means an old wreck of a vehicle; actually old American school buses are used. It was crowded and the driver had a radio blasting the most appallingly bad Mexican music I'd ever heard. The bus, as all of the type, had hard seats and was as bumpy as a wheelbarrow with square wheels.

Around the front of the cab were multi-colored hangings, saints and a large, garishly framed mirror. In it I saw a thin, haggard-looking man, with an unshaven face, messy hair and pale-as-death face. What a mess, I thought. Then my eyes widened and I looked again. It was me! Oh well, I thought, so I've got troubles. Since leaving Mexico City I had decided not to shave any more anyway, as I was planning to grow a beard during the jungle trip. I sat watching the scenery go by, until about two hours later we pulled into Tehuantepec, but I got off before the center of town.

Someone had said there was an agency for car parts near by. I walked about a kilometer across a field to it, waited a half hour, and was told they didn't have any parts for a '55 Rambler. Their parts only went back five years to 1959.

Walking toward Tehuantepec, I saw a shop off the road, and inquired to see if I could get my car fixed anywhere. This was the place, they said. I had hopes now. They sent for the *jefe*, the boss.

An hour later he arrived, and I met the man who was to become my friend for five days. Jorge Sagrero. He was thirty-five years old but was getting paunchy, and looked older. He said he fixed generators. When I told him I didn't have it with me, he said we'd have to go out there to get it and bring it back. I told him that's what I had in mind, and how much would it cost? He said not to worry, he'd make me a good price, so I agreed. I had little choice, but instinctively I trusted Jorge. I liked the way he talked. I found out later he was also a Veracruzano (like Ralph in Mexico City) and had now been in Tehuantepec five years.

At eight P.M. Jorge, two of his helpers and I got on the Oaxaca bus, arriving at El Camarón at ten-thirty. None of us had eaten, so we went into the only *comida* in town, had tortillas and *choritos* (small sausages) and then went to work on the car.

Jorge directed his two assistants, taking over every now and then. The boys, both about thirteen or fourteen, were his apprentices and he insisted they do the work in order to learn. When everything was checked, Jorge made the final tests and gave his judgment. There was no doubt, he said gravely, the generator must be rewound. After taking it out, my crew of mechanics waited several hours with me patiently, joking and swapping stories. At two in the morning a passing truck gave them a lift back to Tehuantepec and I went to sleep in the car.

A few times during the night, the loud grunts and squeals of pigs woke me up. There must have been a dozen of them roaming around town and especially around my car, which was a new object for their attention.

When I got up the next morning they were gone. I hadn't gotten a chance the day before to take stock of the town, so I took a walk around. It was very small and was composed of a general store on one side of the road and the *comida* building on the other, with a dozen small houses scattered around them.

Everyone was already up, but no one spoke to me. They just looked. I was a curiosity, obviously gringo, but not looking very prosperous, to say the least. I walked to the other end of town to a bridge. I asked a small boy the name of the stream below. He said it had none. I walked back to the *comida* and got my canteen full of water and crossing over to the general store, bought some *pastelles* (pastry-bread cookies). But they had no bread or milk.

I went back to the car and dug into my frame pack. I mixed some powdered milk, and made a sandwich with peanut butter and the *pastelles*.

Jorge had said the night before that he would be back at eleven this morning. I expected him between noon and two in the afternoon. Time has little meaning in Mexico. The best way not to get disappointed is to always tack a few hours on to any given appointment, and hope for the best. It was only nine o'clock so I decided to strike up a conversation with someone. I bought some peanuts and offered some to a likely-looking man in his twenties. He was friendly, but with that built-in shyness of most Mexican Indians.

I decided to see if I could get my machete sharpened while I waited for Jorge. My new friend said he would do it, and we walked a few hundred yards, out past the bridge, to a hut on a hill. There he introduced me to his wife and small son and started to work on the machete. He used only a large stone he had placed on the ground. I didn't think it would do much good, but I didn't want to hurt his feelings so I let him go to it.

He kept at it for two hours before he gave up. The machete was almost as dull as ever. He wouldn't accept my money, so I gave him a pack of cigarettes.

Back at the general store, we sat on the steps eating peanuts, smoking and talking. No one knew the name of the stream at the edge of town. It was at least thirty feet wide and it must have a name, I insisted. They insisted its only name was *El Rio* (the river). I gave up.

Noon came and passed. One, two, three o'clock, came and passed. Still no Jorge. I was beginning to wonder if he'd left me in El Camarón for good. Although it was seventy-five miles from the Pacific Ocean, the name El Camarón means the Shrimp. I asked if there were any *camaróns* in El Rio. Everyone laughed. Of course not, they said. How then, I asked, did the town get its name? *Quien sabe?* they said. The story is probably lost in time.

At four-thirty Jorge arrived with Raoul, his number-one apprentice. I was happy to see Jorge, and he apologized for being a *little* late. In fifteen minutes he had the generator in. We pushed the car down a grade, it started, and amid hurrahs we were off for Tehuantepec. But not for long.

We only got a half kilometer up that long incline and we started to buck like mad. I had to stop. Jorge was in the midst of cursing and checking the engine when once more the Mexican Patrol passed by and stopped.

They held a long conference with Jorge, checked and rechecked. Finally the true cause for the bucking was found. A loose valve. Jorge fixed it, we started up, and drove five kilometers to make sure, the patrol following us. I thanked the patrolmen, signed a paper stating how they had helped me, and they left.

Giving Jorge a slap on the shoulder and with a happy *amigo de mi vida,* which amused him no end, we started out for Tehuantepec, arriving just after eight in the evening, and twenty-four long hours after I had left it the night before.

6 · AMIGO, DE MI VIDA

IN TEHUANTEPEC I parked in front of Jorge's shop. It was an old wooden shack, attached to another one. Jorge told me I could leave the car there when I told him I would be sleeping in it. Inside the shop it was bare except for a few car parts hanging on the walls. Jorge only wanted eighty pesos, or less than seven dollars, for all his time and work. I paid him and decided to give him a few gifts. I gave him a Spanish-English dictionary, a blue sports shirt and my two-sided shaving mirror. He liked the mirror best.

The shop was a few hundred yards from the bridge over the Tehuantepec River. We walked over it, and with Jorge's help I cashed my last traveler's check at a clothing store. Then we took a walk around the *zocalo* square. This was the hub of town. All streets and roads converged into it. I was surprised at how small this famous town was.

All around the *zocalo* were stands of food and drinks, all were attended by women. Tehuantepec is a matriarchy. The women work while half the men sit around lamenting their situation. In Tehuantepec the woman is boss, or if not, at least she is treated as equal as men. In Mexico this is unique.

Jorge and I sat down and ate at one of the stands, many of which have large tables. The woman who ran it was as businesslike and outspoken as any man. The food was good. We sat around talking after we ate, and I told Jorge I was low on money and wanted to sell my outboard motor. He said no one would buy it here, but in Salina Cruz, ten miles away, on the Pacific Ocean, someone might. Walking back to the car, he told me we'd drive down tomorrow and try our luck. He invited me to lunch the next day as he left for home, and I agreed.

The next morning I figured my expenses more accurately. I really did need more money. The motor would help; I might get seventy-five dollars, but I needed more. It is against the law to sell a car from the States in Mexico. If you drive one in, you must leave with it. I didn't yet know about Guatemala, but it was my only chance. When I had paid Jorge the night before, I had only a few dollars in pesos left. I had cashed my last twenty-dollar traveler's check and was still 500 miles from Guatemala, where I *might* be able to sell the car. If not, everything was lost.

It may seem foolish that I got myself in such a fix, knowing what my expenses would be and leaving short of money as I did, but if I hadn't left when I did, I might never have done so. Anyway, with all the equipment I had to sell, I couldn't really starve—and there was always the car. All in all, I was glad to have made it this far.

Before noon I went to Jorge's house, which I had some trouble finding, and met his family. He lived with his wife and mother and had two small daughters and a baby son. His wife was a handsome woman and both she and his mother were very pleasant to me. The girls were quiet at first, but later lost their shyness.

After a good meal, Jorge and I walked back to the car and drove to Salina Cruz. We asked several shopkeepers and others if they wanted an outboard motor. No luck. Finally, just when I was about to give up, a car dealer said he'd look at it. We put it on a barrel of water and with little trouble I started it up. I asked a thousand pesos. The car dealer walked away. I asked how much he wanted to pay. He said 700 pesos was his top price. I started to take my motor and leave. After a short but stubborn ritual of sale, we agreed on a price: 800 pesos (sixty-four dollars). Acting like I was giving it away, and telling him so, I took the money. Actually it wasn't a bad deal at all, for a seven-and-a-half Mercury, eight years old.

Jorge and I went to a cantina and had a tequila and beer in celebration. "*Amigo*," I said, starting a toast to him. "*Amigo de mi vida*," Jorge interrupted, laughing. I insisted on giving Jorge ten per cent of my good fortune. At first he refused, but finally I persuaded him and he accepted. Then we walked down to the beach to see the Pacific Ocean.

The sky was a pale blue, the ocean a deep blue and the beach a wide expanse of tan sand, with huge waves crashing in on it. The wind kept whipping sand violently against us, but I set up my tripod camera, put on the self-timer and took a shot of Jorge and me.

Back in Tehuantepec I picked up my machete, which someone had sharpened, and my laundry, which a woman had washed for me. I had supper with Jorge and his family and later he showed me his prize *gallo de peleas* (fighting cock). He had several. Tying one of the champion's legs to a pole, he pitted another against it. They fought furiously for half a minute, but Jorge had to take the untied rooster away before the champion seriously hurt it. He brought out the set of razor-sharp spurs he attached to the legs of his cocks when they fought, pointing out the ones the champion had used in a dozen battles to the death. Although there is an official ban on cockfighting in Mexico, it is not strictly enforced, and thousands take place each year.

A cockfight is a fight to the death, ending when one or the other dies in a shower of blood and feathers. In many remote areas of Mexico, it is a much larger sport than bullfighting. Most villages can't afford to slaughter bulls, so the cocks take on the task of entertainment. Movie houses are slowly sup-

planting both sports, but I predict that some day the last such
contest will not be a bullfight, but a cockfight.

As I was walking into Tehuantepec to mail some post-
cards, Jorge asked me when I was leaving. I said tomorrow
morning, and told him I'd enter Guatemala by way of Tuxtla
and Las Casas. Jorge told me he'd never been to Chiapas state
and that he would like to come along. I told him it would be
great to have him accompany me to the border, and it was
settled. We would leave together in the morning.

I woke up early the next day and walked to Jorge's house.
We had breakfast, took a few photos and at seven A.M. drove
out of Tehuantepec, the station of XEU chiming us out with
its constant station breaks of the first four bars of White
Christmas. It seemed strange to me, with the temperature already in the eighties.

By now everything was *de mi vida* (of my life) between
Jorge and me. I was in good spirits lately, as I was nearing my
objective, and Jorge was a naturally happy type. I would pick
up the canteen and take a drink, saying, "*Agua, de mi vida,*"
and handing it to Jorge, who would drink, saying, "*Cantimplora* (canteen) *de mi vida,*" and laugh. In this light mood
and driving along slowly, for the car was still shimmying now
and then, we drove through Juchitán and kept going east.

Near Zanátepec Jorge noticed several large white birds in
the trees along the road. He said they were called *gorza* and
were fairly rare. When we reached Tapanátepec, it occurred to
me to ask Jorge what the names of these towns meant, as they
all ended in *tepec*. He said he wasn't that familiar with the old
Zápotec language, but that he knew *tepec* meant hill. There
was a difference of opinion as to the meaning of Tehuantepec,
he said. Some claimed it meant hill of the fires, and others said
it meant hill of the tiger. In any case, I said, *tepec* was hill, and
at least that was sure. Jorge said nothing was sure in Mexico,
and I had to agree.

By noon we reached the intersection for Tuxtla and headed north into the mountains. It was a gradual, steady ascent for fifty miles, until Ocozocoáutla, where the road leveled off somewhat. We bought a few tortillas and continued on, arriving in Tuxtla Gutierrez, the capital of Chiapas, an hour before sundown.

Jorge was enjoying his adventure no end. He had a shine from a boy on the steps of the cathedral and admired the passing girls. We inquired about an inexpensive hotel and checked it out. The price was ridiculous. I told the manager his prices were as high as New York and although Jorge tried to reason with him, we finally left, deciding to sleep in the car. We drove it up to a likely spot in the main square, right in front of the Army Headquarters building. I asked a captain if it would be all right to park there all night and he said yes.

By now the neon signs of Tuxtla were all lit up. It was quite a sight, and Jorge spoke of it proudly. After supper I told him I wanted to buy a sombrero for my jungle trip. Jorge took command like a general. He strode down the street asking directions and talking to everyone.

Finally we found the market street and went into a hat store. I described what I wanted and the owner showed me several styles. They were all too small. I was beginning to feel like a giant when he brought out a beautiful hard-straw wide-brimmed sombrero, with chin strap. I tried it on and it fit just right, so I bought it. Jorge said I looked good but like a *bandido*, with the hat and my week-old beard. We decided against a movie, took a walk around town and went to sleep in the car early.

We left Tuxtla after daybreak the following morning, and arrived at Chiapa De Corzo, hungry for breakfast. Chiapa was the first town in Chiapas to be settled by the Spaniards. We drove down a street off the highway which had huge, rough cobblestones. Parking next to the old cathedral, we went around the corner and into a small plaza. It was as beautiful as any I've ever seen, with a small fountain in the middle and a marketplace along two sides. The women were already showing their wares, mostly vegetables and fruit. We crossed over to a small *comida* and had breakfast.

Jorge wanted to see the cathedral, so we went into it. It was huge but empty, being partly under reconstruction. We found the caretaker and asked him if it was possible to get to the tower. He showed us the way, collecting a few pesos admission.

We followed a tight circular staircase to the top. The stones were ancient and worn. I counted the steps out of curiosity: there were sixty-three. The bell platform was a total wreck. We stepped carefully across broken and rotting timbers to a huge bell. It was dated 1576.

The view of the town, small as it was, and the surrounding mountains was beautiful. Descending the staircase, I took another look at the market outside.

In one short hour, Chiapa had become my favorite Mexican village. I imagined spending a few months there, painting, sketching and just relaxing. There was even a small ruin in the vicinity, but no one knew its exact whereabouts. Not having time to explore, we left. My destination was still ahead.

Again the road began to climb, the air not warming up. At eleven, we arrived in the cobblestoned streets of Las Casas, with the imposing official name of San Cristobal, Ciudad de las Casas. The town is almost 7000 feet high, and it was cool and damp. The sky had clouded over and it looked like rain.

I pulled into a yard where there was a mechanic and looked at the front end. The nylon cord was holding fast, but a bolt had fallen out at another point. The mechanic said that was adding to the shimmy I had. I told him to fix it, saying I wanted to fill my canteen and would be right back. Jorge said he would stay with the car.

Before I left, I asked the mechanic about rain. Both he and his helper ignored the low, overhead scud clouds and assured me it was not going to rain. They told me it was the middle of their dry season and hadn't rained in months. I took their word and my canteen and left. In a small grassy plaza I found a fountain. I filled the canteen and headed for the main plaza. I went into a bank and had some pesos converted into *quetzales*, Guatemalan money.

There I met Betty Buchanan, an American writer living in Las Casas. I told her my story and she invited Jorge and me to supper. I accepted. As we talked it started to rain. It was a cloudburst; it came down as if it was the last rain of all rains. After a half hour it let up and I trotted back through the streets to the car.

At the yard where the car was, Jorge and the mechanics were standing under a shelter along the side. We all laughed about the rain, and because I was soaked. Finally it stopped and Jorge and I went to meet Betty in the square. She introduced us to a retired U.S. Army colonel, Ray Cinelli, and we all went into a bar for a drink of tequila. That night we had supper with Betty, and later took a walk around town.

The next morning, Ray invited us to breakfast, at his apartment overlooking the central park. Later we said good-by to Ray and Betty and started on our last hop toward the Guatemalan border.

The road to Comitán was lined with volcanic rock. When we arrived there we only stayed long enough to eat lunch and buy some things I needed. The last fifty miles to the border were full of curves and the pavement was broken and rough. At three in the afternoon we reached it at Cuauhtemoc.

There was only a customs inspection building on the left and a place to eat on the right, where Jorge and I had a farewell beer together. Lifting our bottles, we toasted: *Amigo, de mi vida!*

I waited until Jorge got a ride back to Comitán in a passing car before I said good-by. Then I gave him bus fare back to Tehauntepec, which he accepted as a parting gift.

I clasped his hand and said, "*Adios, amigo.*"

"*De mi vida,*" Jorge added, smiling. Then he got into the car, and was gone.

7 · THE CHRIST OF EL TAPÓN

AT THE MEXICAN customs station, they had three *aduana* (custom) checks. First they checked my smallpox card, then my passport and lastly I went out with a man who was supposed to check the car and its contents. He must have decided it was too much trouble, so we went back inside. There he said something to an official behind the desk. The official told me that the inspection officer did not think it was necessary to inspect my car. I thanked him and started to leave, the officer with his back to me, but I was called back. The man behind the desk explained that the officer could not ask for money, but that if I gave him something, he probably would not find it necessary to inspect my car.

Now that I had gotten the message, I took out a Guatemalan *quetzal* (equal to a dollar) and put it into the inspection officer's hands, still clasped behind his back. Without a word he glanced at it, put it into his pocket and I followed him to my car. There he became friendly, talked about the weather, asked me where I was going in Guatemala, smiled and asked for cigarettes. I gave him a pack of Mexican Casinos, he shook my hand and bid me good luck. I drove off.

A few hundred yards down the road, the pavement ended. I was surprised. I had been told by all that it continued into

Guatemala. It must have been a technicality, because actually I had crossed the border and *was* in Guatemala. Down the road a ways, I stopped at the first Guatemalan customs check. They looked at my passport, stamped it and said *Muy bien*. I was so pleased that they hadn't asked for money I gave them a postcard I had of New York City. They thanked me and, pointing out the next customs check, smiled me on my way.

The second Guatemalan customs check was a large wooden building on the left side of the road. It took me over an hour to get through that one. They unloaded my gear, checked everything, sprayed my tires and again looked at my passport.

The Mexican and Guatemalan governments are known not to be on too friendly terms. When I asked about the spraying, they said they sprayed the tires to keep Mexican bugs out. Also they named this border crossing El Ocotal, so as not to have to use the Mexican name, but actually there is no town on either side.

At five P.M. I was ready to leave. The customs officials asked me if I would give a man they knew a ride to Huehuetenango. When I said yes a tall thin man came up to me. He said his name was Adalberto. He had strange eyes and shook my hand without another word. He was dressed in well kept but old clothes, and had a small sack in one hand.

We started down the narrow dirt road going along at twenty miles per hour in second, as it was rough going. My passenger was soft spoken, very polite and had a strange way and look about him. He almost never spoke unless I asked him a direct question. During the whole time he was with me, this is all I learned about him: he was a Guatemalan; he went around to out-of-the-way Indian villages; sometimes he preached Christianity and sometimes he gave medical help.

As we went slowly along in silence, except for the rattles of the car, the sky began to cloud over. I asked my friend if he thought it would rain. He said it hadn't rained in a month, but would soon. Fifteen minutes later it began to rain like mad.

We were approaching one of the worst spots in all of Latin America, a fifty-mile stretch of road through a mountain valley along the Rio Selagua. It is called *El Tapon*. In Spanish *tapon* means a plug, stopper or bottle cap. Used as an idiom, it means a blocked passage. El Tapon is known for landslides and water streams, which cascade from the mountains that tower around it when it rains, and flow across the road.

We reached El Tapon at dusk. After a few miles, on a long curve bearing left, we saw a car stopped up ahead. A Guatemalan Army colonel was in it with some friends. In front of his car was a mass of dirt and boulders with a stream of water washing through it. There had been a landslide, he said, and we'd have to wait until morning to get through.

My passenger disappeared toward the slide. I got a flashlight and followed him. I found him at the edge of it, ankle-deep in water, staring. I asked him if we'd have to wait as long as the colonel said. He didn't answer. I waded into the torrent of water and rubble and began looking around. I found a spot where a car might get through, but the water would have to recede a bit first. The gravel was five feet high with fair-sized boulders in it and the water was flowing two feet deep over that. It was a hundred feet across.

We returned to the colonel. My passenger told him that the rain would soon stop and a car could make it through in about an hour. The colonel insisted that even if the water stopped now, we'd never clear enough of the boulders away to make it through before morning. He stated emphatically that he had checked it himself. My passenger stated flatly that the rain would stop in a half hour and went back to my car. In the meantime a Volkswagen had pulled up behind us. I explained the situation to the couple in it and said I was going through in an hour.

A half hour later it stopped raining. I waited another half hour, squeezed past the colonel's car, while he tried to order me back as if I were one of his soldiers, and stopped in front of the slide.

The rubble of dirt, gravel and boulders had now washed down to a few feet with a foot of water still pouring over it. My passenger got out and, striding into midstream, said he'd show me the way through. He waved me on. I put the car in low and started through, but in the middle got stuck and began to slide toward the cliff on the left. There was a 200-foot drop to the river, but somehow I wasn't scared. I kept looking at my passenger, who was now across the slide and waving me on, and fighting my way ahead, I finally slid and bumped my way through.

Taking courage, the colonel tried, and got stuck. We went over and helped him push his car through. Then the Volkswagen, in a glorious effort, made it through alone. We said good-by and started down the road.

Soon I noticed that my gas tank was low—lower than it should be. I got out as it started to rain again. The tank had taken a bad dent and was cracked and leaking. I had some Weld-it in the glove compartment. After a minute I managed to stop it completely. We continued on our way, my passenger as silent as ever.

In the next few miles, we passed over two different slides, each about 300 feet wide across the road, but neither as bad as the first one. Later, with the rain continuing and the road deep in mud, full of curves and steep little inclines, we got stuck a half dozen times, sliding back to the bottoms of these hills. At times it looked impossible. But I insisted on not giving up and with my passenger's help we managed to make each incline. He would get out and find a rock. I would start up the incline and get to a point where I wasn't moving forward any more. Then before I could slide back in the mud, he'd put the rock under a back wheel. On one particular slope we did this seven times before I gained the top. I was now constantly in low gear, and by dint of unyielding tenacity we managed to slide along that muddy road into Huehuetenango. It was ten o'clock and still raining.

Thanking me, my passenger got out. I said it was I who should thank him and would he be O.K.? He said yes, wished me luck and started down the street in the rain, carrying his little sack. As I watched him disappear into the night, it struck me how Christlike the man was, and I suddenly realized I didn't even know his last name. Just Adalberto, which in Italian means, *to Albert.* A strange coincidence; or was it?

I never did see the other two cars that we left at the first slide in El Tapon, or ever heard what became of them—and without Adalberto who knows what would have happened to me in El Tapon? I went to sleep in the car, wondering.

8 · QUEZALTENANGO

The following morning I woke up at daybreak. The rain had stopped. I drove to a gas station and while they gassed the car up, I changed into my jungle clothes in a toilet. I was told that the dirt road continued to Quezaltenango, where the pavement started again. That was seventy miles away. I began the trip.

The road turned out to be worse than the Tapon. It was much wider, but it was in unbelievably bad shape. I had to weave my way along it, trying to find a passage, as the rains had cut two- and three-foot gulleys in the soft mud. In other places it was as hard as rock and strewn with boulders. I could see it was being worked on, but at a slow pace, with the rains constantly ruining most previous work.

I finally reached one place where the road made a long descent into a valley, continuing up the other side along a mountain. I started down. It became muddier as I went. At the bottom I saw a group of workmen, busily engaged right in my path. There were truck tracks which I stayed in as I went down, through mud as high as the top of the wheels. I pushed the horn button but no sound came out. I knew if I stopped now in the mud, I'd never get out. I bore down on the workmen. At the last second they saw me and jumped aside as I splashed and slid through that river of mud. I almost didn't make the hill on the other side, but dropping it back into low I finally climbed up it to the top.

There were some beautiful views along the way, but with the constant struggle on the road I had little time to enjoy them. Some spots were so bad they made the car jounce violently up and down no matter what I did. I was usually forced to creep along at five or ten miles an hour in low. Sometimes I shifted into second and hit fifteen, but the road and my heap were not made for that sort of reckless speed. I kept getting out to check the nylon rope holding the front end together. How it held I'll never know. But it did.

The last twenty miles were a mad dash of fifteen to twenty miles per hour in second gear. I may have hit twenty-five once. Then about five miles from town the pavement began. By that time I was so used to the dirt road I didn't care.

I pulled off the road into a town plaza that had a fountain, and filled my canteen. A man parked nearby in a jeep said hello. He asked where I was going. I told him. He said he'd show the way as he was going there himself. I followed him through the small town and down a highway for miles.

At noon we arrived in Quezaltenango. In Quiche Mayan, *tenango* means place of, and Quezal is a short form of Quetzal, the Guatemalan national bird; hence Quezal-Tenango—place of the Quetzal bird. The ancient Mayan name for the town, Xelajú (pronounced Shell-ahú), is still used by many people, and by all the Indians. This name, in huge white letters, can be seen on a hill near the north end of town.

Suddenly the jeep I was following stopped. The man got out and introduced himself as Belarmino Monzón. He asked how long I'd be in Quezaltenango. I told him only long enough to sell my car, if it was possible. He told me I could sell my car, as he knew it had been done, but that the *impuesto* (customs tax) would be high. Even so, I said, I would be glad, as I needed the money badly.

I only had four *quetzales* to my name. Belarmino said hotels were expensive, and he knew a family that might put me up for a few days.

I followed his jeep several more blocks, until we came to a stop across the street from a long building. That, he told me, was the *impuesto* building, and there, he said, pointing to a doorway marked *avenida* 8, c-09, were his friends.

He rang a bell on the door and soon a small Indian girl opened it. He asked for the señora. A minute later she came. Belarmino introduced me to Celia de Wiegand, a woman in her late thirties. He explained my situation, and she said that certainly I could stay there, as long as I needed to. I thanked Belarmino and he left.

Inside the doorway was a beautiful little courtyard lined with flowers. The house was on the right. Upon entering, I saw that I was just in time for lunch, and the whole family seemed to be there. Washing up and trying to make myself presentable, I re-entered the dining room. The señora introduced me to her son Felipe, who was twenty-one, her daughter Hilda, twenty-two, and her son's wife Argentina, eighteen.

The food was excellent and everyone was friendly and interested in my trip. I told them about it briefly and my intention of going into the *selva* (jungle). They were impressed. After lunch I was given a room off the courtyard, with its own entrance. It was perfect. I told Felipe about my intention of selling the car. We drove it into the courtyard, unloaded my gear and then went across the street to the *impuesto*.

I told the officials that I wanted to sell my car, and asked what the *impuesto* would be. They checked my passport and the car's registration and went through several large books. Finally they came up with an astounding answer. The *impuesto* would be 525 *quetzales* ($525). I couldn't believe it. I explained that the car was ten years old. They insisted that the tax figure was right. I pointed out that the car only cost a hundred dollars in the States. They thought that was a good price, but that had nothing to do with it. A tax is a tax. I asked Felipe what I might get for it in town. He said probably 550 *quetzales*, maybe 600. I refused to leave. I kept insisting that something was wrong. Then to get me out, they showed me the official tax book for cars being sold in the country. When I saw it in black and white, I still couldn't believe it.

Finally I left, muttering half in English and half in Spanish to Felipe that it was all ridiculous. I was disgusted. Felipe agreed that it was ridiculous and that I should be angry. But, he said, the law is the law. He was right, but then I thought of something. For every law, especially one like this, there is always a loophole. That afternoon, by accident, I found it.

A Guatemalan lieutenant was calling on Hilda. In talking to him I mentioned the difficulties in selling the car. He said that there was only one way to avoid the *impuesto*. How? I asked. If a Guatemalan officer buys it, and if he goes to Guatemala City, and if the officials there grant him a waiver of *impuesto*, then, he said, you can sell it with some sort of profit. That was the loophole. Now I had a chance.

That afternoon, in a happier mood, I cleaned the car, decided what I would leave in it, and what I could give to Felipe, and rearranged my jungle gear again.

After supper that evening I found myself so exhausted I went to bed at ten o'clock. Before I did, I took the last reading of the car's speedometer and checked it against my starting mileage. I had come 4740 miles, or 7584 kilometers. That, I thought IS a long drive.

The following day I had to wait until Felipe had his lunch break from work before he could take me to the army headquarters outside of town. Having the whole morning with nothing to do, for the first time I had a chance to study the family.

Hilda was blond, tall and definitely German-looking; quiet, polite, she talked less than she thought. Felipe's wife, Argentina, was small, with a typical Spanish-Indian face. A Latin to the core, she was by turns shy, excitable, naively forward or pensive, but usually she was smiling or singing off alone in a corner. A sweet and pretty thing, I soon began to call her *Lindita* (little pretty one). The others all thought that was very amusing.

The señora appeared to be mostly of Indian stock, but she later proudly told me her father had been Italian. Her maiden name was Bernasconi. She was a typical Latin mother. Proud, commanding, in full control of the household, outspoken, outwardly religious, friendly and hypocritical—a natural, unaware actress and, naturally, overdramatic. But I liked her. She was happy to recite her troubles, so I soon learned of them.

She had married a rich German immigrant when she was still in her teens, just before the Second World War. When the war came he was called back to the fatherland for duty. When the war ended, with Germany defeated, all his land and property were confiscated by the Guatemalan government. On trumped-up charges, which she didn't care to explain, he was refused permission to come back to Guatemala. Saving some of his estate, she managed to buy this house and raise her two children. Some years before, she had received news from Germany of her husband's death. Felipe, married only a short time, was working in an office to lighten the load.

I even got to talk to the Wiegands' shy Indian maid. Eluvia Escobar was a small girl of twenty-five. She had been given out to the Wiegands for a sum of money by her father on a five-year work contract. Everyone in Guatemala has identification papers, but hers were being held until her contract was terminated. She could not leave town, and although she wasn't supposed to leave the house she did the family shopping. Eluvia worked from five in the morning until nine in the evening, got five *quetzales* a month for expenses, plus room and board. That's one aspect of civil rights; in Guatemala.

That afternoon after lunch, we jumped into my car and Felipe showed me the way to army headquarters. There I climbed the steps of the building and announced to the guards at the door that I was selling my car, and that if anyone was interested to spread the word. I waited.

Soon several Guatemalan officers drifted out and down the steps. They were mostly colonels and captains. One fortyish colonel in particular was interested, and seriously. I was asked many questions by the others, but he just looked at the car, in and out, and occasionally said something. He was a short bull of a man. After everyone had left, he asked *quanto?* (how much?). I said 300 *quetzales* and he said 200 and that was it. He refused to budge. I had no alternative, so after a while we shook on it.

"*Va bien*," I said. "*Dos cientos.*"

It was done. But there were other consents to be had. The colonel told me that he would have to go to Guatemala City Monday to see if he could get the *impuesto* dropped. It was now Saturday. He told me to meet him back at that spot at noon that coming Tuesday. I agreed and left.

The following three days were spent in rearranging my jungle gear once again, taking walks down to the main plaza of town and visiting the marketplace. The park in the main plaza was not large but it was beautiful. The marketplace was exceptionally large, and the items for sale quite inexpensive.

Much of Quezaltenango is built on the side of a hill, and the streets, many cobblestoned, wind up it to the park. It is the second largest city in Guatemala, with a population of 50,000.

The food at the house was always plentiful, good and with much variety. Besides the usual fare of beans, rice, tortillas, potatoes, chicken and beef, there were such dishes as Spanish omelettes covered with stewed tomatoes and onions, cabbage omelettes, fried platanos, fish dishes of all kinds, soups of all taste and combinations, a variety of cheeses and tropical vegetables and fruits of all sorts. The Wiegands enjoyed eating, and Eluvia the maid was a good cook.

When someone left the table he would say either *Muchas gracias* (many thanks) or *Boñ por véchio* (good in behalf of old age: a trilingual phrase of French, Spanish and northern Italian dialect. How it came about in Guatemala is a moot question), whereupon those still seated would answer with the phrase not used.

I always spent a few hours after supper, which ended at eight, talking with the family. One night the girls, Hilda and Argentina, sang Spanish songs to me for an hour. They were surprisingly good. When they finished they asked me to sing an American song. At first I declined, but when they were so persistent I thought it only fair so I sang, *I Can't Get Started*. Then we got the señora to sing an old Indian song. It was a pleasant evening.

On Tuesday I met the colonel who wanted to buy the car

at army headquarters. He had good news. He had gotten permission to drop the paying of the tax. The deal was sealed again with a handshake. He had an army mechanic test-drive the car and then we went to a lawyer.

The lawyer spent an hour asking questions and finally had his secretary type up a four-page document, which stated all the particulars of the sale. I had been told I would need this document to leave the country without my car. The colonel paid me with two 100-*quetzal* bills. It didn't seem like much in exchange for the car, those two pieces of paper, and besides I had to pay the lawyer his twenty-dollar fee. But I was solvent again.

At eight that night at the house of Señora Celia V. de Wiegand, I had finished packing my jungle gear. I was leaving my suitcase and such civilized gear as extra shirts, pants and underwear there. I had decided that if I could come back to get it without too much trouble I would. If I didn't it was no great loss. The suitcase was an old battered B-4 bag, and everything in it was old too.

I was taking two bags with me—my army frame pack, containing mostly personal items, and my jungle hammock. I also had a burlap bag, which held the rubber boat and most of my food. On my pistol belt hung a twenty-two-inch machete, two pouches and a pair of small binoculars. Over my khakis I wore a heavy O.D. jacket.

As Felipe had a car, I gave him all the things I had taken out of mine, such as the hydraulic jack and the spare tire. To the señora I gave three blankets. I paid her the one *quetzal* a day room and board she asked for, plus two for good measure, and slipped one to Eluvia the maid. I was ready to leave.

I said good-by to the family and they all wished me good luck and hoped I would return safe and soon. Then Felipe took me to the bus station in his car. At eight-thirty I left on the Lima lines first-class bus for Guatamala City.

Everyone had numbered seats, but the bus was half empty, so I lay across the back seats and tried to sleep. I kept dozing off but occasionally a swerve of the bus would wake me up, and before dropping off to sleep again I'd stare up in the blackness, thinking about what lay ahead of me. It is a 200-kilometer trip, through mountain country, and at midnight we pulled up in front of the bus station in Guatemala City.

I asked the bus driver if I could sleep in the bus the rest of the night. He said it would be O.K. as he and a few other passengers were doing the same thing. I went down the street, and two blocks from the station came upon the main plaza park, all lit up, deserted and lonely. Further along it, three soldiers in battle dress, with rifles slung, were patroling in the middle of the street. They watched me pass, with my Mexican sombrero and my machete slung, but said nothing. Very pleasant, I thought, for a police state. I walked the width of the park and went into a cafe. I found the toilet, had a coffee and pastelle, and then returned to the bus and went to sleep.

At six in the morning a tolling bell woke me. I got my bags, had the station attendant call a taxi, and left for Aurora airport. The plane I wanted for Poptún was scheduled for seven o'clock, but I knew it would be late. The ticket was eleven eighty-eight, and I was allowed thirty-three pounds. My bags weighed 103 pounds together and I thought the four-ninety they charged for seventy pounds' overweight was reasonable. I was right about the plane and had time for a leisurely breakfast.

Just before eight o'clock, the plane, an old twin-engine DC-3 (C-47), taxied up outside the Aviateca building. (Originally built without seats as a cargo plane, the old C-47 was the original "flying boxcar" that flew over "the hump" of Burma in the early forties.) My brother Rico, a former army airplane mechanic, says that if the engine parts are replaced, these planes will fly forever. He's probably right. The last one was built over twenty years ago, and some are closer to thirty years old.

Together with about twenty other people I boarded the plane. The rear was jammed full of cargo and baggage, and up forward there were thirty-odd bucket seats in double rows on each side of the aisle. The whole plane had that well-worn, cluttered look, which shows practicality, and gives you a re-laxed feeling of confidence. In a matter of minutes we took off. If you've never been in a twin-engine plane before, let me tell you this: you really know you're flying.

We climbed steadily and headed north over the brown, eroded-looking mountains of central Guatemala. Forty-five minutes later we were over them and landed at Chahál, on the edge of the jungle. I got out and stretched my legs. Cargo was being dropped off, and a group of Indian women and children stood around as some men helped the crew unload. Minutes later we took off and rose over the trees until the jungle below became a low-hilled green carpet. Soon it could only be seen as patches of green, between the drifting white and gray clouds. The engines droned on, and every now and then we'd bounce along through an air pocket.

Thirty minutes later we came down through the clouds and the man next to me pointed out through the window. "*Eso es*," he said. I looked out and saw a plain ahead covered with houses. Suddenly the old DC-3 banked sharply. I grabbed my seat. We straightened out, dove low over the trees and headed for a long red-brown strip of earth carved through the jungle.

We were dropping fast and the dirt runway seemed to be rushing up to meet us. Finally we hit, and I was surprised at how smooth the landing was.

I was the only one getting off. My bags were dropped down to me and a few minutes later I was standing there with them, watching the plane taxi down and take off. I watched my last link with civilization roar out over the jungle and disappear. I was alone. I had finally reached my destination, but it was only the end of the beginning. This was Poptún.

Part Two

Into the Jungle

1 · POPTÚN

ACCORDING TO THE research I had done on the area, there was a ruin near town; it was even listed on one of my maps. What I needed first of all, however, was a place to drop my bags. Then I would hunt out the ruin.

I looked around the airstrip and spotted the radio shack. Two boys were standing outside it. I called them over and asked them about the ruins and a hotel. They answered me with a series of *Si-si's*, got a wheelbarrow and loaded my bags on it. Before I knew what was happening, we were off on a dirt road. I asked if we were going to the hotel and they just smiled and said *si*. When I asked how far the ruins were, they said they knew of no ruin. Was there a ruin at Poptún? they asked. Yes, I answered, Poptún has an ancient Mayan ruin. Pushing the wheelbarrow, they had a short discussion on the subject. I missed most of it. Then one turned to me and said, "*No. No esta ruinas a Poptún.*"

I told them there was a ruin, as it was shown on a map I had. Still, maps in the tropics have a peculiar habit of fabricating towns and rivers and jumbling names and, at the opposite extreme, of simply leaving them out. I silently began to wonder about mine.

We went around a bend in the road and came upon a street with houses. Most of them were wooden shacks, with poled sides and thatched roofs. Some had board sides and some even had corrugated metal roofing, but almost all were painted in the most brilliant and astounding combinations of colors. Greens and pinks with blue trimming, yellow and blue, blue and green, white and blue and pink, purple and yellow with red. The combinations were inexhaustible, and somehow they all went together. The Mayan painter is a genius.

The boys stopped at a corner house and unloaded my bags, saying this was the place. I didn't know what they meant, but I paid them something and went inside anyway. It was a store selling odds and ends, mostly candy and fruit, and not much of either.

I asked the señora inside about the ruin. She knew of no ruin. I asked about the hotel. I was in luck. There was one hotel in town. Then she told me that her husband owned a truck and maybe he knew about the ruin. He was returning soon, she said. The relation between owning a truck and knowing of the ruins may not seem apparent, but I knew exactly what she meant. In these areas of the world, where almost everybody has nothing (and earns only slightly more than that), anyone who does own a car or a business usually does know everything. Or so it appears, in comparison to what the other people seem to know.

I decided to stay and meet the man. The woman told me he also owned the store, the house behind it and the house next to it. This, I thought, on top of a truck? He must know something! I was right.

Sometime later, when I had gone outside to look at a huge poinsettia bush that was covered with large scarlet bracts of flowers, a truck pulled up. A man got out and introduced himself as Señor Aldana. I asked him if he knew where the ruin of Poptún was. He said he had heard of one, a few kilometers outside of town, and knew its approximate location. He was taking some people to another village, Santa Barbara, fifteen kilometers north up the road, and would pass the spot near the ruins. If I wanted, he would drop me off and of course I accepted his offer and thanked him. He drove off and returned a while later, his bus-type station wagon loaded with people. I threw my bags on the roof luggage rack and got in.

When we reached the spot where Aldana thought the ruins were, he stopped. "Somewhere in there," he said, pointing into the jungle to the right. I got out and two men got off with me. They took my bags off the roof and appointed themselves my friends and guides. They were both drunk. I told them to put the bags back on the truck as Aldana would return in three hours to pick me up, but they shouldered the bags anyway and headed into the jungle. The truck drove off as they did so.

I watched it go off down the road and turned to look at the drunks staggering into the bush with my packs. There I was, with two drunks and two packs, neither of which I wanted, trying to find a ruin of which no one knew the location.

I caught up with my "guides." We had gotten about ten paces into the jungle when one of my unwanted crew who was carrying the bag containing the boat and food, threw it off his back and slammed it to the muddy ground.

I shouted, *"Que haces, amigo? Estas loco?"*

He began to curse at me in Spanish. It was too heavy, he yelled. His friend up ahead came back to break it up. I relented. Angrily I shouldered the now muddied bundle myself, and started off.

Poptún is located on a low plateau. Surrounding the town for a few kilometers is a plain, which although mostly jungle is interspersed with occasional areas of grass; in these there are tall pine trees. A strange combination of jungle-forest vegetation, this is what they call high-jungle.

In ten minutes we reached such an area. I told my drunken companions to wait there for me and proceeded to scout around alone. Drawing my machete, I cut three paths into the jungle, each about a hundred meters deep, first straight ahead, then left, then right. When I had found nothing anywhere and it started to rain I decided this was probably not the spot where the ruins were, and certainly not the time to go on.

Returning to the drunks, I found them as happy as two ducks, sitting on my bags in the rain. I put on my poncho and directed them back to the road, where I decided to wait for Aldana and try the ruin another day.

When we arrived at the road, I saw a man on horseback, down the road a way. I called to him several times and finally he turned and started back toward us.

When he reached us, I asked him if he knew where the ruin was and was surprised when he said yes. I asked him to lead me there, and we started off, he on horseback and the two drunks trailing us with my bags. A motley crew.

We continued along the path I had made, through the grassy area and beyond. My direction had been right, up to a point. We kept bearing left, until finally my new friend dismounted and started to slash his way deeper into the jungle. The rain had stopped. After about two kilometers, he stopped and informed me we had reached the base of the pyramid, but I could see nothing. I introduced myself and my new guide said his name was Rafaél Castellanos Válles.

I began to question him about the ruin, while we rested

before making the climb. He said that the ruin had been cleared of bushes and trees under President Juan José Arévalo, fourteen years ago, but it hadn't been tended. Now it was completely covered again. (I later learned that Edwin M. Shook and Robert E. Smith had been the archaeologists.)

When we were ready to start, the drunks said they weren't coming. I asked Rafaél if his horse and my bags would be safe with them. He said yes, he knew them; they drank but they were not thieves, he assured me. We started the climb. As I looked back for the last time, I saw one of the drunks lift a bottle to his mouth and take a long pull. It was the last we saw of them.

Rafaél took the lead. The underbrush was thick, thorny and tangled with vines, and the machete work was heavy. It soon became apparent that we were indeed on the side of a pyramid. The handcut stones underneath shifted and slid, and all in all it was a rugged, steep climb of about 300 meters. It took us a good half hour to zigzag our way to the top, which was somewhat clearer of brush and trees. I began to inspect the construction.

I found that two sides had terraces flanking it, while the top center platform was about seven feet higher. These sides had good remains of two stretches of the platform walls, each about thirty feet long. The terrace was fifteen feet wide, and the center platform close to seventy feet long on each side. The other two sides were completley overgrown, crumbled and impossible to inspect. The view from the top, when one could manage a look through the trees, seemed to place us surprisingly high. It began to rain again.

Across the steaming jungle below us and about 400 meters away, I noticed another "hill." Rafaél said it was another pyramid. It was as high as the one we stood on, possibly higher.

These two pyramids were exceptionally large, and I estimated the height of the one we were on at no less than 200 feet, a giant for a Mayan structure. The highest ever discovered, Temple IV at Tikal, in the Northern Petén, is 229 feet high, and there are four other large temples at Tikal with the following heights: Temple I, 155 feet; Temple II, 143 feet; Temple III, 178 feet; and Temple V, 188 feet.

These are all exceptionally high. Most Mayan structures are under 100 tall. Moreover, the 229 feet of Temple IV at Tikal includes the height of the temple on top of the pyramid's central platform, and the ornamental roof-comb. In further comparison of size, Temple IV at Tikal, from ground level to the top of the center platform on which the temple stands, is only about 150 feet high. Obviously if there had been a temple on the pyramid I now stood on, it had long since crumbled and vanished. But with the added height of such a temple, if it ever did exist, Poptún would have had the highest temple pyramid ever constructed in the Mayan Empire. I speculated for a minute on its possible height if it also had a roof-comb, and using the Tikal pyramid-temples as a guide, came up with the astounding figure of 320 feet. Even considering that my estimation of the Poptún pyramid may have been off slightly, it still must have been one of the largest ever built.

It was still raining, but I insisted on setting up my tripod and camera on the terrace. I set the timer and took a photo of Rafaél and myself in front of one of the center platform walls. I took a few more photos, and then in the rain we cautiously descended my first Mayan pyramid.

On the way down, Rafaél pointed out a plant he called *yerba del monte* (woodland grass), and said that when the roots were boiled and the juice drunk it cured snakebite. I didn't mention to him that there are two kinds of basic snake venom, colubrids and vipers, with opposite effects, as he probably had no idea which it would cure.

The colubrids are represented in Guatemala by the coral

snake. The vipers include the tropical cascabels (rattlers), bushmasters and the fer-de-lance. Now the colubrid victim is shocked in the nerve centers. His blood cannot coagulate, becomes watery and often breaks out through such places as the eyeballs. On the other hand, the vipers' venom coagulates the blood and destroys the corpuscles. As I said, I didn't mention any of this to Rafaél. In any case, I figured that even if I knew which venom it counteracted, by the time the stuff was boiled and ready to drink, I'd be dead.

Snake venom, unless stopped, circulates through the entire blood stream in about a minute. By then it's already too late. After that, venom effect varies, death usually occurring any time between fifteen minutes to one hour. The only sure way of treating snake bite is still to slash the fang marks, suck out the blood and venom and apply a tourniquet. After that, you can start praying.

We reached the bottom of the pyramid and found Rafael's horse and my packs. The drunks were gone. Returning on the trail we had cut, we reached the road in a heavy downpour. I thanked Rafael and gave him a quetzal. Then I sat down under a tree, watching him ride off down the road in the rain, wondering if I had missed Aldana and the ride back to Poptún. Ten minutes later he arrived from the direction of town. He said he passed by a half hour before, and luckily for me he had to return to Santa Barbara. I got in and we went off down the road in a heavy rain.

After a ten-kilometer drive we reached Santa Barbara and I got off. Aldana said he would pick me up in an hour. I told him I was thinking of going down the *rio* alone. He told me he didn't think it was a good idea and drove off. I crossed the bridge across the Rio Santo Amelia, put my bags under the eave of a house and waited for the rain to stop.

Some small boys came up and we talked for awhile. I asked if any of them knew anyone who could tell me about the *rio*.

They said they would go around town and ask, and left me. I checked the river. It was only thirty feet wide and hardly moving. Soon the rain stopped and the boys returned. They had found the man who could tell me about the *rio*. Helping me with my bags, two of the boys crossed the bridge with me and entered a blacksmith shop on the opposite side.

I was introduced to Rigoberto Zelada, a heavy-set, fairly dark man, about five foot nine, who was in his late forties. He said he had been on most of the rivers of the Peten, but that this one was *torcido* (cursed). One of the worst. He said the name on my map was wrong. The *rio* was not called the Santa Amelia, but the Machaquilá. He said some people who lived near it, where it enters the Rio Pasion, call it the Santa Amelia, but that is not its name.

I asked him if he'd ever been on it. He said no one had traveled on that cursed *rio*, but from all reports of *chicleros* (chicle gatherers) and other sources it was an impossible river to navigate. He explained that it went underground a few kilometers downstream for an undetermined distance, and that when it emerged again it was full of rapids, cascades and *tapóns* (fallen trees across it). He asked why I was interested in the river.

I said I intended to go down it alone in a rubber boat, to search for ruins. He strongly advised me not to go; especially not alone. *"Es suicidio!"* he said.

I knew he had a point, but explorers are optimistic by nature: otherwise we wouldn't be explorers, we'd be something else. Like clerks. Of ruins on the Machaquilá, Zelada knew nothing. I thanked him and left.

The *rio* intrigued me. Here was an explorer's dream. A virgin river. Unexplored, unnavigated, wild, virtually unseen by man. And to add to the mystery, it had the reputation of being *torcido*—a cursed river. I couldn't resist the challenge, and on the spot decided to go down it—but not alone.

While I had been talking, Aldana had returned and I saw him down the road by his truck, talking to a man. I walked over to them and was introduced to José Antónío Golíb, a pleasant man in his thirties. I soon got on the subject of the purpose of my trip. Golíb said he had traveled through the *selva* (jungle) in search of ruins, and had worked with Franz Blom for three years.

From my research on Mayan explorations, I knew that Blom had been one of the most active and respected explorers in the entire Mayan area. Moreover, Golíb informed me that he *had* heard of a recently discovered ruin down the Macha-quilá, although he had never been there. He told me that a man named Enrique Valdez, back in Poptún, knew its loca-tion. The challenge had turned to expectation!

I thanked Golíb, and Aldana and I drove off to Poptún. He dropped me at the only hotel in town, the Sac-nite, which in Mayan means white flower.

Standing out front was a U.S. Army major, who intro-duced himself as Larry Lawrence. He told me that Poptún had about 1500 people and a Guatemalan army barracks just out-side of town, with a few U.S. Army advisors. He himself was stationed in Guatemala City, but as an army engineer had come up to give his advice on something. I went into the hotel to arrange for a room.

There was one set of rates. One quetzal a day for a room and seventy-five centavos for each meal; or a flat three quetzals daily for room and board. I was given a padlock and key and shown to a door. I carried my bags in. It was a six-by-eight-foot room with wooden walls and a window. All that was inside was a cot and a small table with a kerosene lamp on it. As for privacy, the wooden walls ended three feet from the ceiling and were screened the rest of the way.

Outside, between the two rows of ten rooms and the en-trance, was the dining room with three wooden tables and some chairs. To one side there was a storeroom and, out along the backyard a roofed-over, open-sized kitchen. A shower room and outhouse building were at the far end. The whole structure was roofed with corrugated sheeting. It was the largest building in Poptún.

That night I found out that a few generators around town supplied current for a few street lights and a few houses and buildings, the hotel being one of them. The lights came on at six and went out at ten. After that it was flashlights and kerosene lamps.

At six-thirty supper was served: meat, potatoes, tortillas, beans and coffee. Simple but good. Besides me there were only the major and an American, John Martin, at the hotel. Martin was a big man in his fifties. Quiet and discreet, when he did speak his voice was loud and commanding and he tended toward philosophy. But he was pleasant. The kind of ex-patriot you've seen in those tropical places in the movies of the thirties. Like Thomas Mitchell. Martin ran a general store next to the hotel and was a permanent resident.

The owner of the hotel was Juan Francisco Rivera, but everyone called him Don Paco. Small, unconcerned, he had a pencil mustache and was in his forties. He didn't talk much, but I liked Don Paco.

That night I went for a walk around town to look it over, and see if I could find Enrique Valdez, who was supposed to know where the ruin on the Machaquilá was. The streets were muddy and the street lights shone like dim solitary beacons, here and there. There was a large building down one street, where occasional dances were held and, on Wednesday and Friday, movies shown. Almost no one was on the street.

I found Valdez' house after several inquiries. His wife said he was unloading a ship at Puertos Barrios, and bringing cargo from it to Puerto Mendez. He would be back late that night or the next day.

On the way back to the hotel I was stopped by two men in uniforms. They had .45-caliber pistols slung on their hips. They said they were town policemen. They seemed to talk casually, but after a few minutes managed to find out everything about me: where I was from, what I was doing there, how long I intended to stay and so forth. Then they looked at my passport. When they heard I was going into the *selva*, they asked me if I had a rifle. No rifle? A pistol, then? No pistol, I said, smiling. Thinking about the one that was bulging in my shirt-front pocket, I decided it was time to leave. They asked me if I didn't think it would be dangerous to enter the *selva* without any firearms. I said no, I had my machete. They laughed. After a few more words, we shook hands and I left.

I knew that pistols were absolutely forbidden in Guatemala, as were all rifles except caliber twenty-two. A hunter might get permission to carry in a thirty-thirty, but he would have to take it out with him. I had taken special care not to mention my pistol to anyone. Pistols were, in all cases, taboo.

When I reached the hotel, the lights went out. I lit the kerosene lamp and looked through my pack, checking items, maps, thinking about how it would be. In the dim yellow light of the lantern, visions of the jungle began going through my mind. The jungle fever was mounting.

The following morning I checked to see if Valdez had returned. He had not. I went to see Aldana. He said that a man called Carmen Acté knew something about the Machaquilá river area and might be able to help me. Someone went to get him and he arrived awhile later.

Carmen Acté, a soft-spoken man of forty, had obvious Mayan features. He told me the following story of Machaquilá.

In 1957–59, geologists working for Union Oil had made tests in the region south of the river. Carmen said he and Valdez, together with a dozen other men, had cut trails for these men and supplied them with food. I asked Carmen if they had used the river. He said that once they tried to transport supplies down it in an aluminum boat, but after capsizing several times, abandoned the idea. How far had they gone? Not far, he said, probably no more than thirty or forty kilometers. And what of the ruins? He only knew that they were about halfway between Poptún and the Rio de la Pasion, but exactly where he couldn't say. He had never seen them. About how far would halfway to the Pasion be? I asked. By land, he estimated, it would take upward of ten days to cut a way there. And by river? No one uses the river, Carmen said seriously. "*Es torcido.*" The geologists learned that, he added. And who actually discovered the ruin? I asked. "*Quien sabe?*" he said: Who knows? But it wasn't Valdez.

Apparently Valdez knew no more about the river or the ruins than Carmen did. I asked Carmen to go up to Santa Barbara with me and talk to Golíb. He agreed. Early that afternoon, Aldana drove us up.

Golíb as usual was smiling and talkative. He didn't know what Valdez knew about the ruin, or who had discovered it— only that Valdez had mentioned it to him once. Golíb offered to come with me, but couldn't be sure he'd find the ruin, even with Valdez. In any case he was tied up with lumber work and would soon be off in the *selva* for a month. I said that was too late. Still, he insisted in telling me about other ruins that we might visit, when he returned. He mentioned a ruin, without name, three days' march southeast of Poptún. Was it Pusilá? I asked. No, he said, but near it. Golíb was impressed with my knowledge of ruins. How did I know of them? From books, I said. He laughed. Books are no good in the *selva*, he told me, only guides. Then he continued. There were *ídoles* (idols, meaning the stelae) at the ruin. But a better ruin was in the opposite direction, to the northeast.

Twenty miles north of Poptún was a village called Dolores. North of there, he said, was a known ruin called Ixcun. About ten kilometers east of Ixcun was the Rio Mopan. He said if you followed it eight or ten kilometers up the right side you would come upon an unrecorded ruin, also without name. Golíb said he had found it while looking for chicle some years back. He said there wasn't much there, but one very unusual stella. He said it was huge, about five meters high (sixteen feet) and had a three-foot-tall figure carved in the center. This figure he said, almost whispering, had a belt carved on it, and in the middle of the belt was a *morado* (purple) stone, which he described as being roughly eight inches in diameter. Worth *mucho*, he said. The charm of Golíb and his ruins was irresistible but I couldn't wait a month. Moreover, Machaquilá was even more fascinating. I thanked Golíb again and Carmen and I returned to Poptún with Aldana.

On the way back I asked Carmen about Golíb's stories. Carmen, an unimaginative type, thought the stories too embellished, but he wouldn't state whether he believed them or not. Who can say? I for one chose to believe them. Naturally.

That night I again went to Valdez' house. His wife again told me he would return *mañana*. Leaving with apprehension and impatience, I took a walk through town. There was a full moon out and the many tall poinsettia bushes, covered with hundreds of flowers, gleamed in the moonlight with that singular lush, tropical red.

Back in my hotel room, I repacked my entire frame pack, in preparation for a trip that seemed as remote as ever. I was becoming disheartened.

The next morning, Carmen came by and told me Valdez had returned from Puerto Mendez, which they here call La Cadena (the chain). We went to see him.

Enrique Valdez was a really nice chap, medium height,

mid-thirties. He said he was sorry but he didn't know where the Machaquilá ruins were either. Besides, he had to return to La Cadena in a few days.

I refused to give up. Did anyone in town know? Were there any other men from Poptún who had worked with the geologists? Carmen and Valdez thought awhile. Then Valdez asked Carmen about a man named Pablo. Carmen said that Pablo had worked with the geologists too, and he lived in town.

I thanked Valdez, and Carmen took me to see Pablo. We ended up in a water-logged section outside of town. Turning off a lane, we went through a banana grove and came upon a house.

Carmen went inside. A minute later he came out with another man, whom he introduced as Pablo Paredes. Carmen had already mentioned my plans. Pablo told me that *he* had discovered the ruins, but couldn't remember if it was in 1958 or 1959. Could he still find them? I asked. He said he could. In fact, he had taken another *gringo* there two years before. He didn't know his name, only that they called him Don Juan. (I later learned that the man's name was Ian Graham.)

As for going to the ruins, Pablo assured me that the river was *torcido*, and that it would be best by land. He also said he had never even been in a boat on a river, and didn't know how to paddle. Could he swim? I asked. Yes, Pablo answered. Good enough, I said, and gave him my plan.

I wanted both of them to go with me on the trip. Who could get hold of a mule and a rifle? Carmen said he owned both. I told them my intention was to march to the river, at a spot well beyond the underground section, with the mule. From there Carmen would return with the mule and Pablo and I would continue down the river to the ruin in the rubber boat.

It was the middle of the rainy season, Pablo said; and Carmen shook his head. I continued, saying I would pay each of them a guide's pay of three quetzals a day, plus two a day for Carmen's mule. I had doubled the ante of the standard going rates.

"*Vamonos?*" I asked.

What I was asking them to do was to go into the jungle in the middle of the rainy season. On top of that I was asking Pablo to go down an unexplored, treacherous river which he believed to be cursed. They looked at each other and then at the crazy gringo, who had originally planned to try it alone. Finally Pablo spoke.

"*Vamonos!*" he said. I smiled. Carmen agreed and asked when.

"*Mañana,*" I said. "*Mañana? Bien,*" Carmen said, and "*Bien,*" Pablo echoed.

We shook hands with an *Hasta mañana,* all around, and I left, my brain in a whirl of thoughts.

That night in town I met Carmen and Valdez and we talked about the morning trip, over a few bottles of *indita* (an anise-base drink). I returned early to my hotel room feeling quite happy, and before I dozed off to sleep I had visions of slashing my way through the jungle, of conquering the Rio in a few days and entering the jungle-shrouded city of Machaquilá. It was a fairy tale, but fairy tales are easy to believe when one wants to. Especially with the help of *indita.*

2 · . . . AND SO IT BEGINS

I WAS UP in the morning at daybreak. And in my little room while the roosters crowed, I checked my bags for the last time. I had two. The large frame pack and the *pita* bag. (I had since learned that my "burlap" bag was not that at all, but made of pita, a type of sisal hemp). This bag now held not only the rubber boat but a pair of aluminum oars, rubber pump, ten-inch rubber boots, sketch pads, two one-pound cans of powdered milk and other food rations, including fifty Nu-V bars. Three or four of these bars will sustain a man for a day. My frame pack contained the usual array of items. I had made a list of everything in it that morning and put it in one of my outside shirt pockets for reference. It read as follows.

IN MAIN POUCH:

    1 jungle hammock
    24 one-ounce tropical chocolate bars, in tin can
    56 Nu-V bars, one and a half ounce each
    16 packs cigarettes (wrapped separately in plastic)
    1 battery lantern
    3 12-ounce cans corned beef and 1 can Spam
    4 cans sardines
    2 6-ounce cans cheese
    1 half-pound box Bolton biscuits
    1 Woodsmen emergency kit
    1 two-ounce jar instant coffee, w/plastic cup
    2 3½-ounce cans of pemmican
    1 pint Irish whiskey
    box of sundry items, containing lighter fluid, extra flashlight batteries, first-aid dressings, multiple vitamins, salt tablets, halazone tablets (for water purification), extra still and movie film.

IN TWO SIDE POUCHES:

    1 can antiseptic spray
    1 can mosquito spray
    1 small bottle Listerine
    16 mm. movie camera

hunting knife with 6-inch blade
10 nickel packs of Kleenex

IN TOP COVER FLAP:

1 towel
1 mosquito head net
1 pair extra socks
2 pair jockey shorts
30 plastic bags

Tied on the outside of the frame pack, I had a shave-kit bag containing other sundry items, such as soap, medicines, snakebite kit, etc.; a waterproof rubber flashlight and fifty feet of quarter-inch nylon rope. The pockets of my shirt and pants were crammed with such things as passport, .32 Browning automatic pistol, pen-light, Swiss army knife, ballpoint pens, billfolds, cigarette lighter, scotch tape, etc. Inside my shirt I carried my F 4.5 Ansco Speedex camera.

I was wearing a pair of army battle pants, khaki shirt, fatigue jacket over that and low-cut boots. On my pistol belt hung my twenty-two-inch machete, a hunting knife with eight-inch blade, two pouches filled with medicine, a compass and halazone tablets. I completed my outfit by slinging my two-quart canteen and putting on my Mexican sombrero. I was ready.

After a light breakfast, I had the cook make me six hard-boiled eggs which I put inside my shirt. Then I stood outside the hotel and waited for Pablo and Carmen.

At seven they arrived with Carmen's mule, which he called Alcira. I watched them lash on my packs, and theirs. The morning was cool and cloudy, with a chill in the air. At seven-thirty we started out of Poptún, heading west.

Carmen, his rifle slung, took the lead with Alcira and set a brisk pace. We walked through open grass fields speckled with pine trees, and every now and then a small *cerro* (hill) would appear on one side or the other. Pablo claimed these were not *cerros* at all, but small ruin mounds. At one point, Pablo cut a piece of wood from a dead fallen pine tree; he called it *ocotel*. He said it was the only thing that would sometimes start a fire when the wood was wet.

We continued for four kilometers across this plain, reaching our first arroyo, a small stream, after an hour. Awhile later it started to rain as we reached and entered the jungle on a muddy trail. The trees were tall but the underbrush was not thick. Inside the jungle, it was much darker than it had been outside on the open plain. We soon passed a single house which Carmen called *El vano de los cocos*, the hollow of the coconut palms, and there were in fact a few coconut trees around it. We continued deeper into the jungle on the three-foot-wide muddy trail, which my guides kept calling *el camino* (the road), and soon reached the second arroyo, which we waded through. The rain continued.

Our trail was surrounded by innumerable types of trees. There were tamarindos, with their thin, spreading roots; chapai's, with spiny trunks; and of course the stately, tall red-barked ramon. I spotted a few of the huge, beautiful corozo palms, and many types of tropical palms and ferns unknown to me.

By eleven o'clock we reached the Rio Concomá, thirty feet wide and full. We followed it a way and then headed back into the jungle. Our trail was now muddier than ever, and we slid through mud at times a foot deep. Alcira, the mule, kept a slow steady pace and seemed to have no trouble navigating this river of mud. I did; it stuck to my boots like glue, and at one point, trying to pull my boot out of a particularly gluey spot, I lost my balance and ended up on my backside in the slimy muck.

After awhile we reached a series of rocky passes and had to step our way cautiously through each one. They went up sharp for fifty feet and then down again. This went on for an hour. Then we leveled off again and continued along on the flat jungle floor.

Suddenly Carmen stopped short. Pablo ran up and held Alcira and I saw Carmen moving slowly up ahead on the trail. Then he brought his machete down into the mud several times.

"*Que pasa?*" (What's happening?) Pablo called to him.

"*Coralita,*" Carmen said, and continued on. As we passed the spot where Carmen had stood, I looked down into the mud and saw two pieces of the red-ringed coral snake which he had killed. Farther on we ran into six-feet-tall, thick and tough *zacate* grass, which continued on and off for a kilometer or more. It was hard to cut and between this and the other underbrush it was slow going.

We were heading for the Kekchi Indian village of Concomá, where we arrived just before one P.M. There were three thatched houses with pole sides in an irregular clearing. The largest was about fifty feet long and twenty-five feet wide. Carmen knew the head man at Concomá and went into this long house to see him. He came out with a short stocky man and introduced him as Santiago. He was quiet but polite, and invited us into his house.

Inside the atmosphere was cozy, with a dim light filtering through the cracks between the poled sides. Hammocks were slung out at either end and also at one end was a stone fireplace where two women sat cross-legged, de-graining corn.

We talked of our trip, had some coffee we were offered and each ate an orange, of which Pablo had brought a small sack. Some other Indians entered and I passed out vitamin tablets to all. Everyone smiled and swallowed them without a word. It appeared to me that these Indians looked more Mexican than Guatemalan, but they had that quiet, unsmiling resignation of the Guatemalans. I estimated this village to be twenty kilometers (thirteen miles) from Poptún.

Leaving Concomá, we headed out on a trail that went north and, after awhile, swung west again. The trail was becoming dimmer. There was less mud but more machete work.

By midafternoon we again reached the Rio Concomá; it was sixty feet wide, and this time we would have to go across. Carmen and I found a huge fallen tree across it and walked over, but Pablo had to take Alcira the mule through at a two-foot-deep ford he had found, some fifty meters downstream.

As we continued along the trail on the other side, the rain, which had stopped for a few hours, started up again. Pablo told me that in another five or six kilometers we would come upon a *ranchera*. We plodded and sloshed our way ahead for an hour in a heavy downpour. Then we came to an arroyo and waded through knee-deep. A hundred meters on the other side we came upon the *ranchera*. It was just a ten-by-fifteen-foot two-sided lean-to. It was stacked with dozens of rows of ears of drying corn.

There was a huge clearing in the jungle before it. Carmen said it was the jungle *milpa* (cornfield) of the people of Concomá. The so-called *ranchera* was actually a corn shed.

We started through the *milpa*. It was harder going than the trail we had been on, a tangle of bushes, vines and fallen trees. Alcira the mule was having a tough time. The cornstalks were hardly visible in this *milpa*, and at times the tangle of bushes and vines were ten feet high. I said we should go around it. Pablo told me that the trail ended at this cornfield and that the jungle was much worse than this. The *milpa* was several hundred yards across. It seemed like a mile. After almost an hour we had gotten through, and now stood at the base of a solid wall of trees: the jungle.

It was four-thirty and the sun was just going down. Carmen said there was no use entering the jungle now, as it was already dark inside. He advised that Pablo and I return to the *ranchera* with Alcira, while he made a cut into the jungle for the following day. He started to hack away at what appeared to be an impenetrable wall of branches and leaves, and Pablo and I led Alcira back through that disaster of a cornfield. On the way back Pablo took a photograph of me on a huge stump of a ramon tree.

Once we were at the *ranchera* again, Pablo unloaded Alcira. The mule happily shook its back and started to eat grass. We put our packs in the shed and Pablo started a fire. It was then I noticed the mule's back. On its left side Alcira had a wound. The skin was gone and a bloody spot was swarming with mosquitoes. I cleaned it, swabbed it with iodine, to Alcira's distress, and taped a gauze bandage over it.

By five-thirty darkness had fallen and Carmen had returned. Pablo had a cloth full of tortillas and we had them with my hardboiled eggs and coffee for supper. Then we talked about our trip.

Pablo estimated we should reach the Rio in a day and a half, possibly two. After that, he figured a three-day river trip to the ruin. I added an extra day for good measure. That made it six days to the ruin by the river route. Carmen said that the land trip was safer, but probably would take a few days longer. With the mule, he said, it could even take ten days, as a mule trail has to be made clearer than one for men. I only had food for ten days, which could be stretched out to two weeks, but that was it. Besides, I was also low on money and had my heart set on the river trip. Both men tried to dissuade me and insisted the land trip was better. But I stuck to my guns. Six days by river to the ruins. There, I told Pablo, he could return by land to Poptún or continue with me down the Machaquilá to the Rio Pasion.

Pablo was undecided. A land trip alone through unknown

jungle was very dangerous. I told him that from the ruins to the Pasion could not be more than four days, as it was the halfway point. That made it ten days. The Pasion was a large river with no waterfalls or blockages, and from there we could float to Sayaxche in no more than four days: a total of fourteen days. To return back through the jungle, I said, was impossible. Not impossible, Pablo said, but hard and dangerous.

"Then we go all the way to the Pasion by Rio," I said. "*Bien?*"

Pablo would not commit himself.

That night Pablo and Carmen wrapped themselves in their hammocks and went to sleep on top of the piled corn. I had slung my hammock across the front of the shed. I stayed up awhile, sitting by the dying embers of the fire, then stepped out to have a last smoke and think about the mystery of the jungle around us.

It was almost silent, but not quite. Faint sounds, movements, could be heard. A huge *ramón* tree stood nearby, its 100-foot trunk rising straight, into a silhouette of tangled branches. From here west lay thick unknown jungles, the cursed river and an ancient ruin, lost in a tangle of tropical growth.

It started to rain again as I zipped myself inside my hammock. I lay there listening to the rain and trying to imagine what lay ahead in the jungle. This was the end of the trail. Beyond lay the unknown.

3 · CAVES

THE NEXT MORNING was cool. I looked through my netting and saw a low mist rising over the *milpa*. The sky was cloudy. I got up and found several large rats rummaging through our packs on the ground. I chased them off and started the fire. Alcira was already eating grass, and Pablo and Carmen soon got up. We ate, loaded Alcira and left.

On the far side of the *milpa* we entered the trail Carmen had cut the night before. It was more like a tunnel. The jungle was so thick you couldn't see more than seven or eight feet. An eight-foot jungle. If a red blanket were hung nine feet away, you wouldn't see it. After a hundred meters the trail Carmen had cut ended, and he started slashing away at the jungle again. Every now and then Pablo took the lead. He was looking for the trail he had cut with Don Juan two years before, but there was no trace of it. I was in the rear position but even so occasionally had to slash at branches myself, so thick was the vegetation.

We continued on like this for at least a kilometer and then the underbrush began to clear considerably. You could now see at least twenty feet through the leaves, and the machete work was only normally heavy. Occasionally the jungle cleared to such an extent that I could easily see a hundred feet away. There was a series of these strange jungle clearings, and I asked Pablo about them. He knew no explanation. He said that there are places like these in the jungle, but that he had never seen so many in such a small area.

Pablo and Carmen were both forty-two years old and both had been *chicleros* (chicle hunters) around Poptún for twenty years or more. Pablo said he had been in this area hunting chicle trees, but only a few times. Carmen also said he had hunted chicle there once. Now, for the first time, I took a good look at my guides. *Chicleros* are supposed to be tough and dangerous. Stories about their escapades, usually including murders, circulate the Peten. For a moment I wondered about my guides, but I soon decided that they were OK and tried to forget it. Anyway I had no choice. There I was.

As we went on through light jungle, I thought I saw something through the trees. I asked Pablo if there were anything around there. Like what? he said. Like a hill or a cliff, I said. Pablo didn't know. He had never heard of one. Carmen hadn't either. As far as they knew, it was flat jungle. Then I saw something again, on the same side, to the right. I stopped to take a good look. It looked like a light spot near the top of the trees. The sky was gray and cloudy. Was it a cloud? No, it wasn't moving. I told Pablo and Carmen that I wanted to go over and see if it was a cliff. They asked me why. I said I just wanted to go over and look at it. Actually, I had visions of discovering an ancient cave, with artifacts in it. I did!

I told Carmen and Pablo to wait where they were, and that I would be right back. I cut a course south, in the direction in which I had seen the white spot. After a hundred meters, I could make out something like a *cerro* or hill ahead of me. It was mottled, white and black. Since there is nothing but limestone outcroppings in the Peten, I guessed that it must be a limestone cliff. Soon I could plainly see that it *was* a cliff. Another hundred meters and I had reached it.

The base was rocky and treacherous. The cliff itself was jagged and menacing and overhung in spots. It was about a hundred feet high. I went along it looking for openings. Then I found one. Excitedly I went in, but it ended ten feet inside. I continued along the rocky base, now and then chopping away at the brush with my machete. The base of the cliff turned out to be literally pitted with caves. But none went in further than twenty feet. Then I found one that was probably closer to thirty feet deep. My excitement mounted. Where's the big one? I thought. There must be a big one.

As I went along, the small caves disappeared and a ledge of solid limestone started up along the base, finally reaching a height of seven or eight feet. I couldn't see what was over it. I steadily slashed my way along it until finally I reached a spot where I managed to climb up on top. The ledge was twenty feet wide from the base of the cliff. It was irregular and broken, but had a strange, symmetrical, manmade look about it. I searched it for traces of handcut stones or stucco crumblings, but found none. I continued west along the ledge, in the direction I had been going. It seemed to be turning slowly to the south. Then I came to a place where the cliff overhung to a great degree. I came to a spot where the terrace was twice as wide and went back level to the cliff base. It was like a huge amphitheater carved out of the side of the cliff front. A dark spot back at the cliff base caught my eye—it was an opening. I went over to it.

It was a cave entrance, about eight feet high and six wide. It faded back into blackness. I took out my cigarette lighter and cautiously started in. After twenty feet it had dropped to four feet high, then up to ten feet, then down to four feet again. The width was just as irregular, also varying between four and ten feet. Outside it was hot, maybe eighty-five degrees and humid. Inside the cave it was twenty degrees cooler and even damper.

Then a strange feeling came over me. There seemed to be a pattern to the cave. If it was four feet high, it was ten wide; if it was ten high, it was four wide. The lighter got hot and I put it out for a minute. I was now in at least forty feet and it was pitch-black. The air was damp and rank.

Suddenly there was a sound up ahead. My heart jumped and I crouched down, striking the lighter again. I saw nothing, but I pulled out my pistol anyway. As I went forward slowly, up ahead the cave seemed suddenly to end. I went up to the wall and to the left saw a smaller passageway drop off into the blackness. The flickering light bounced dancing shadows along the walls and back into this void. That strange feeling returned. Then I heard another sound back in the tunnel to the left. My hair crawled on my scalp, and I began to head hurriedly toward the entrance.

Halfway back the lighter went out. I got down and started to crawl toward the faint daylight ahead. My hand touched something as I went along. It felt like a sharp stone. I picked it up and kept going. With relief I gained the tunnel entrance, and stepped out into the white sharpness of daylight. Squinting, I looked down at the stone I had picked up. To my surprise I saw that it was a potsherd (fragment of pottery). It was obviously an ancient piece, and I was determined to go back deeper into the cave, but I needed a flashlight.

I started to retrace my steps along the cliff to return to Pablo and Carmen, and met them halfway back along it. They had come to see why I had taken so long. I said I had found a cave and needed a flashlight. I decided on the six-volt lantern and insisted that Carmen undo Alcira's load, so I could get at my pack. Reluctantly he did it. I was not too keen on re-entering the cave alone. I showed them the potsherd. I asked who would come back and go in with me. Carmen volunteered. Pablo would stay with Alcira.

I took the lantern and Carmen followed me back along the cliff to the cave. At the entrance I cocked my pistol, and with the lantern in my left hand, stepped inside. Carmen was right behind me. The stronger light gave a clearer picture of the cave, but it was still eerie.

We went in as far as I had gone before, but this time I estimated the distance. Sixty feet. I entered the tunnel to the left and after ten feet it again turned to the right. The irregular widths and heights continued, but now it was never more than six feet high or wide. Slowly we went ahead, crouching. Thirty feet after the first turn there was another, again to the left. Again it turned back right, and again the tunnel continued ahead for thirty feet. There at a narrow spot, four feet high and only three wide, the tunnel seemed to end.

A huge stalactite had dripped down over the centuries and blocked the passageway. Around either side of it I could see that the tunnel continued ahead. We were now at least 120 feet from the entrance. In the dense blackness, my lantern only shone ahead fifty or sixty feet, but I saw no end at that depth, so I must assume it goes deeper. How far no one will ever know. I tried to squeeze around the stalactite but I couldn't. I was itching to get by. Carmen suggested that maybe there were *idoles* (idols) further ahead. My frustration grew. I tried the other side of the stalactite. Still too narrow. Again I threw my beam around the obstruction and into the tunnel. This time I saw a movement and a gleam. It looked like a pair of eyes. My heart gave a thump, hesitated, thumped on. In a split second I imagined a Mayan ghost coming toward me out of the darkness. A clapping sound and a flurry of movement at the end of my beam brought me out of it.

Carmen shouted *murcielagos* (bats), as they began to flap and flutter down the passageway right at us. Carmen turned and started out fast. I was right behind him. We didn't stop until we reached the middle of the first sixty-foot stretch. There I could hear the bats way back in the tunnel. It was the sound I had heard when I had first entered the tunnel alone.

Only bats, I smiled at Carmen. Yes, he said, but reminded me they were vampires. He was right; these small bats are the bloodsucking vampires and very dangerous. They have an anesthetic fluid in their bite, so that when they strike you don't feel it. Although they usually attack only sleeping victims, striking at the jugular or big toe veins, they have been known to do so in broad daylight. A vampire bat can suck out almost a pint of blood in twenty minutes, and three or four can drain a man to death in that time. They are not really dangerous if you're awake, but Carmen left the cave anyway. I decided to stay inside and search for more potsherds. I scraped around in the dry dirt of the cave floor. After ten minutes I had found seven or eight.

Outside, I cleaned them off with water. Some of them had

yellow or red-brown designs painted on them, and one was even incised with crisscross markings. Some were thin and some thick. I couldn't tell if they were early-phase *tzakol* or the later *tepeu*, classical Mayan pottery fragments, but they were certainly one or the other, and not less than a thousand years old. If they were early *tzakol* they might even date 500 years earlier.

I showed them to Carmen, who indicated some interest, but when we returned to Pablo he was amazed. He said that I had made a great discovery. The cliff was unknown, and there was no doubt that I was the first man to enter the cave. I had to agree with him. At least, I said, I was the first man to go in for a thousand years.

The cave and surrounding area held many mysteries. Could the jungle "clearings" we had passed through once have been Mayan floored plazas? Could the ledge in front of the cave entrance have been man-made, and was the whole cliff an ancient Mayan citadel? And was there a larger cave some-where along it which held a hidden sanctuary of Mayan carvings and treasures? There was a good chance of all, or at least one, of these speculations being true.

For a minute I thought about searching the cliff for an-other day, but then I had to face reality. I didn't have spare provisions to play with. If I wasted a day, I wouldn't have enough food to continue the journey, without causing a hard-ship. I had visions of Pablo and me starving to death out in the jungle. (At that time I had no idea how close to the truth I was.) Reluctantly I gave up the idea of looking for the larger cave, and we started out again, heading west. We were still a long way from the Rio.

Not far past the cliff of the caves, the jungle thickened to a solid wall of limbs and leaves. It was a two-foot jungle and the machete work was exceptionally heavy. We had still seen no sign of the trail Pablo once had cut. Obviously we were in virgin jungle. After two hours we had gone less than a kilometer. I decided to change our course and head directly for the Rio, hoping that we had now passed the place where it went underground. We began to cut our way north. Early that afternoon we reached its banks, but it was almost dry. We would have to try farther upstream tomorrow.

I scouted for a camp site. It was now three P.M. and the machete work had exhausted us. About a hundred feet off the Rio in the jungle, I found another cave.

Pablo said he remembered this one. He had passed it on his trip with Don Juan. I asked if anyone had gone inside to investigate it. He said no and I asked why. He said he didn't know, they were in a hurry at the time. This time, however, Pablo decided to follow me in.

The entrance was twelve feet high and eight wide, but twenty feet inside the roof sloped down to four or five feet and the width to six, and we had to crawl on all fours. We went in another twenty-five feet, and reached an obstruction, as in the first cave. At this point, two tunnels about six feet long widened around it on either side. I chose the left and barely squeezed through.

I saw immediately that the tunnel went ahead and then turned to the left. It was now only three or four feet high and maybe five wide, and we were only fifty feet from the entrance. Up ahead the tunnel seemed to turn about sixty feet away. Pablo refused to go any farther, but I kept crawling slowly ahead toward that left turn. I kept the lantern on the dirt floor or dead ahead. Stopping for a second to rest, I began to shine the lantern over the walls and roof. I was thirty feet from the left turn.

Then I saw some black objects protruding from the wall on the right. I crawled forward a few feet for a closer look. I thought at first they were bats. Then I thought they might be huge black butterflies. Their wings suggested this. I inched forward. Then I saw a huge leggy thing above the winged creatures. Immediately I thought: *Tarantula!*

I threw the beam of the lantern across the roof and saw several more. Bringing the light to the left wall and back toward me, I saw another dozen. There was no doubt: they were huge spiders—as big as a man's fist, and the closest no more than five feet away! The light had disturbed them. A creepy feeling came over me as they began to crawl around. The bats, or butterflies, began to flap their wings.

I whispered back to Pablo, "*Atrás, atrás, arañas!*" (Back, back, spiders!)

Pablo, well behind me, scurried out around the stalactite. Slowly I pushed myself back, shining my light around the walls. Then I threw it on the roof and over my head. I froze. There were spiders all around me. One small black one was staring me in the face, a foot over my head!

There was no time for panic. Instinctively I gave a shove backward and kept going until I bumped into the stalactite. Turning around, I squeezed myself through and ran into Pablo on the other side. We both smiled.

Shining my light back down into the tunnel, I could see the big spiders slowly crawling toward us, and the "butterflies" still flapping their wings.

"*Vámonos!*" I said, and we crawled out into the daylight.

When we told Carmen what was inside, a discussion ensued. Pablo said the spiders were tarantulas, and Carmen said they seemed more like black widows. I mentioned that they might be both. The ones in the back of the tunnel certainly looked like tarantulas. I don't know of any other spider that is as large as a man's fist, but the one smaller black one over my head did have that black-widow look. Between the spiders and trying to figure out if the other things were bats or butterflies, the subject went on from time to time all night.

Pablo and Carmen wedged some poles in the cave entrance and slung their hammocks right there. I decided I wanted no part of whatever was in the cave. Carmen said they wouldn't bother us but I slung my hammock twenty feet out in the jungle anyway. After eating, we stayed up for a few hours talking, and then being tired from the last bit of heavy machete work, we went to bed. Between the caves and the thick jungles we had encountered that day, we had only covered eight kilometers, and had no idea how far we still had to go to reach the Rio.

4 · THREE MEN AND A MULE

THE NEXT DAY I advised a course parallel to the Rio. After an hour of slashing our way through heavy jungle, it cleared, and the machete work became light again. We could now see fifty feet ahead of us and our pace quickened. I began to take notice of the trees in the area, asking Pablo the names, and taking notes on what he said.

The average height of the jungle was well over a hundred feet, but below this umbrella of tall trees was another stratum of small ones, varying between fifteen and forty feet tall. Pablo said that most of this jungle was of one tree, which he called *el cañshián*. It was a large palm with small leaves. The wood is used in building houses and in carpentry. Then there was a tree that had leaves similar to a hickory, which he called *chechém*. When cut it emitted a milklike fluid. Pablo said that if this fluid gets on your skin, it causes swelling and rashes. In the eyes it can cause temporary blindness and permanent damage.

There were also some *guano* and *coroso* palms. The guano has bracts of ten or more roundish leaves on a stem. The coroso palm is probably the most beautiful in the jungle, varying from thirty to a hundred feet tall. On the smaller ones, huge limbs start out five feet off the ground, and in a bundle flare out for twenty feet or more. The long thin leaves go out at right angles to the limb, looking like a double-toothed comb. When it is taller, the branches may not start for thirty or more feet off the ground and the gently curving branches become forty feet long. Once you have seen a large jungle coroso, all other palms lose their charm. I consider it the queen of the jungle, although the Guatemalans reserve that distinction for the large and sparse *ceiba* tree. We saw one that day, and it was huge. The trunk was over six feet in diameter.

Besides the palms and other trees, there were also spiny and thorny palms, most of them small, but they were dangerous. The *chapai*, for instance, a ten-foot tree, looks like a miniature model of a large coroso. It had eight-inch spines hidden among its palm fronds, and the trunk was solid with the three-inch spines straight out along its entire length. Pablo showed me small clusters of nuts in its branches, which he said were good to eat when ripe. They resembled miniature coconuts, and were in clusters of forty or fifty.

Occasionally Pablo pointed out a *cuerno de toro* (bulls' horn) tree. Every branch and limb has four-inch horn-shaped thorns, at intervals of three inches. I cut some off. They were black, thick and hard as steel; I couldn't break any of them. They are difficult to see on the tree and this makes it particularly treacherous. There was also an occasional huge *sapote mamé* and some *chico sapotes*, the tree from which chicle is gotten.

By late morning we reached the place Carmen called *el corosal*. It was a grove of coroso palms. They were mostly small but still beautiful. The ground was littered with dead fallen branches, which looked like giant discarded garden rakes.

Soon the jungle overhead began to get thicker and the trees larger. We had entered a huge forest, damp and full of giant ferns, where no sunlight penetrated. There was no machete work to speak of. Pablo was unfamilar with the place and said he had never been through this area.

Area of jungle trip map is shown shaded

Alcira the mule, not caring for the fast pace we were setting, constantly kept stopping and munching on bushes and low leaves. Carmen kept calling back, *"Hah mula, segua!"* (Mule, follow!) And so it went all day, the mule ignoring all pleas and threats. Once Carmen became so angry he ran back to Alcira and gave her a hard kick right in the rump. She gave a jump and started out slowly, but didn't learn her lesson. She kept stopping all day.

I say she, because I think of a mule as a female. Actually they're neuter, the get of a horse and a donkey, and cannot reproduce. But if you look closely at one they appear female.

The heavy overhead canopy of trees continued, and as we went on through the humid dark jungle, it began to rise and fall slightly in small hills. Going down one of these slopes, I saw Carmen stop, unsling his rifle and fire into the jungle ahead. Something crashed down through the trees and Carmen went off the trail toward it. He returned smiling with a bird he called *mancolola*. (That is the local name; actually it was a *perdis* bird). It was plum-colored, as big as a small hen, with gray and brown feathers on its underside. He plucked the feathers on the spot, saying that if he waited until later, they would be too hard to pull out. We continued on.

A hush had fallen over the jungle. After awhile, Pablo stopped and pointed out some tracks across our trail. I could see the large cat tracks of a jaguar, but I couldn't make out the deeper ones. Pablo said a *danta*, (a jungle deer the size of a tapir), was being tracked by a *tigre*. The tracks were only hours old and we continued ahead cautiously for awhile. But we neither saw nor heard the *tigre* and his prey.

Farther on I saw my first jungle flowers, brilliant orange splashes against the various greens of the jungle. They were two or three feet off the ground and appeared like a cluster of small lilies, with seven or nine blossoms on a center stem. I made a quick sketch of one.

By midafternoon I decided to head for the Rio again, to see if it was full and above ground. I changed our course to north as before. After a kilometer of medium machete work, we reached it, but again it was dry. I climbed down into the arroyo and, tying Alcira to a tree, Carmen and Pablo followed.

The river bed was extremely rocky, and in spots had stagnant pools of water in it. I found several large snails along the bottom. The centers were red, fading to brown and tan. A few

were alive. Somewhere below us, Pablo said, the underground
Rio was roaring. A few hundred yards along the river bed, there
was a limestone fault, which dropped down ten feet or more.
If the river had been flowing, this would have been a cascade.

All of the Peten area is on a limestone shelf, with a varying
depth of earth over it. The frequent cracks and faults in the
brittle stone let water through, and beneath it the underground rivers form. In this spot the underground stream was
so large it drained the Machaquilá of water, but further ahead
it probably narrowed. This would cause the water once more to
seek the surface and continue out into the river.

I wanted to find this spot and observe this phenomenon,
but Pablo said we had no time to follow the dry river bed. It
was rough going, the limestone being extremely jagged. He
said we could make better time through the jungle. I doubted
it, but conceded when he said the mule could easily slip and
break a leg on the stones.

Climbing out of the arroyo, I saw new flowers along the
banks. They were on strange, beaded stalks, with two large
leaves on either side, and looked something like African vio-
lets. Pablo didn't seem to know the names of any of the
flowers. As if to make up for it later on the trail, he pointed
out a strange, leafless vine growing on a tree. It had bunches of
what appeared to be bright red grapes growing on it. Pablo
told me that these were poisonous to man, and if a dog ate a
few he died within an hour. He said only *faisanos* (pheasants)
can eat them, but that a man can eat the *faisands* meat, and it
is nonpoisonous.

Further on we ran into rocky passes and a few fallen trees.
By the time we cut a way through for Alcira, it was four
o'clock and time to set up camp for the night. Darkness fell on
the jungle at five o'clock, an hour earlier than outside in the
open, and it wasn't light enough to go on the trail until six in
the morning, so we only had about eleven hours for traveling

and thirteen of darkness. First the hammocks are slung, than a fire is built and the packs put near it under the hammocks, and you are ready for the long night.

Carmen gutted the *mancolola*, made a spit and started to roast it. It was ready in a half hour. The meat was tender, with a strange sweet taste, but good. Later we discussed the trail ahead.

Pablo said that we were not far from a place he called *el arbolito*, the little tree. If he could find this, he could get his bearings and lead me to a spot on the Rio where he knew it was full and deep. Up to now, however, he had not been able to find the trail he had cut with Don Juan two years ago. A normal trail, he said, grows in and completely disappears in six months, but the one he had cut was three meters (ten feet) wide. He couldn't believe it was all grown in and neither could he understand why he hadn't been able to find it if it wasn't. It was the first sign of what Pablo later referred to as the *viaje torcido* (cursed trip).

I too had apprehensions. I had estimated a two-day march to the Rio. I was right, but the Rio had still been underground and the river bed dry. Now it was the end of the third day, and none of us had any idea how far off the full Rio lay.

Heavy rain started and we decided to get into our hammocks and sleep. I lay awake for some time thinking about our situation. I could tell that Pablo, whose hammock was next to mine, was not sleeping either. That's the jungle, I thought. Full of the unexpected, mysterious and uncertain, but all the more beautiful. I fell asleep that night listening to the muted sounds of life and movement in the jungle, knowing that man was the intruder.

The next day we had a surprise. We walked into a clearing in the jungle with only small trees in it, and saw a large patch of sky for the first time in two days. Carmen had no doubt that it was the old chicle camp of *Salomón*, abandoned five years before. Pablo also knew of it and now fixed his bearings for *el arbolito*. We started out.

The temperature soon reached ninety degrees and the humidity was extreme. It was to be the hottest day of the whole trip. It may not sound hot for the tropics, but this was the middle of winter in the Peten, and at night the temperature dropped to sixty degrees or lower. With the rains coming two or three times a day and totaling seven or eight hours, the humidity must have constantly hung around a hundred per cent. Everything was wet or damp, and rusting. I oiled my pistol every day, but every day it rusted a little anyway.

We started out in the direction Pablo had set for *el arbolito*, and after a kilometer ran into a series of fairly high, rounded *cerros*. The jungle thinned again on the ground but got thicker at the top level, and became dark and damper, if that was possible. Mosquitoes began to plague us for the first time, and the jungle became a steam bath. Alcira was getting restless, and I was drenched with sweat.

We started up a long, particularly clear slope of jungle, when something stopped us dead in our tracks. Alcira almost bolted. It was a loud guttural roar like a *tigre*, and seemed to be close, maybe a hundred feet ahead and to the left. We all waited. Then there was a loud, deep doglike bark from the same spot. But it was no dog.

I went up to Carmen and Pablo and asked them if it was a *tigre*. No, they said, it was a *saraguate*. The *saraguate* is a large, black, powerful monkey built like an ape. They are three feet tall and dangerous. Pablo said they had a tree with several females in it, which they guard with their lives. If anything comes close, they try to scare it off, imitating the *tigre*. If that fails, they drop to the ground and attack.

Carmen unslung his rifle and I took out my pistol. We skirted the tree while the *saraguate* roared and barked. It sent chills along my spine. Alcira was edgy and Pablo had to lead and pull her along, but we gained the top of the small *cerro*. Then the *saraguate* suddenly dropped to the ground fifty feet to our right and with a loud, tigerish shriek, started to charge.

Alcira bolted and Carmen turned to grab her. Pablo raised his machete and stepped back. It was up to me. I threw my pistol out and fired twice into the ground ahead of it. The *saraguate* stopped twenty feet away, completely surprised. Then it clawed the ground, gave a last roar and ran off back to its tree.

We quickly turned, pushing Alcira down the other side of the *cerro*, which was very steep, and slipped and stumbled to the bottom. There we were trapped. Several huge fallen trees surrounded us. The *saraguate* roared and barked again. He was showing the females he wasn't afraid. Pablo said he might charge again, but was not dangerous as long as we had our guns. If he got too close to you, he said, a machete wasn't much good.

While Pablo and Carmen started to cut a way through the *tapón* of trees for Alcira, I turned and kept my eyes in the direction of the *saraguate's* yells. Fifteen minutes later Alcira cleared the blockage and we left the *saraguate* to his fate. I was glad I didn't have to kill the brave beast.

We continued on through a series of smaller but steeper *cerros* and rocky passes. The jungle was very beautiful in this area. There were huge *ramón* trees, with their five-foot-thick reddish trunks rising one hundred feet straight up and stretching into great leafy branches. Giant gray-trunked *muñeco* trees, *canshians*, *sapotes*, an occasional coroso and giant ferns surrounded us. It was a paradise.

As we started up along the side of a steep rocky *cerro*, I spotted some red spots along our trail. They were small jungle flowers, looking like waxy tea roses, except that the red was a brilliant scarlet, and the centers were blue and yellow. I took a color photo of them.

Further along the rocky pass, there was a sudden loud fluttering in the treetops above us and I saw a large bird fly through them and land. We were all startled. Carmen said it was a *faisano*, but he hadn't seen where it landed. I spotted the bird, called Carmen over and pointed it out. Taking careful aim, he fired. The bird was hit, but only flopped down to a lower branch. Obviously it could not fly away. Giving me a chance, Carmen told me to shoot it down. Instead I handed my pistol to Pablo. I knew he was itching to use it. Pablo took careful aim and fired. The bird didn't fall. Then he fired again. This time it fell straight down through the branches like a rock. We went over to it. It was dead. A huge, fifteen-pound *faisano*, and when Pablo and I stretched its wings, we were amazed to find that it had a five-foot wing span. It had a black back, brown wings and a tan belly. Again Carmen plucked the feathers on the spot. I put a large one in the band of my sombrero and we started off again.

Awhile later we reached *el arbolito*. It was nothing more than a clearer spot in the jungle vegetation, but we were all happy about it, especially Pablo. Now he had his bearings.

From this point he had gone west with Don Juan. We would go dead north, he said, and reach the Rio Machaquilá after about two kilometers. We started out.

The jungle was suddenly very thick and wild, but it flattened out and there were no more *cerros*. We soon came upon a fairly clear spot. In the middle was a tremendous ant hill. Pablo said these ants give a very bad bite. He called them *zompopos* (leaf-cutting ants). I spotted a few. They were a half inch long and quite red.

The hill itself was immense, easily twenty-five feet across and seven or eight feet high. If these ants were the size of a man, I estimated that the construction would have been higher than the Empire State building and over a mile long. Using reverse comparison, the Great Pyramid of Cheops at

Gizeh, Egypt, the largest ever built by man, would only be three feet high. I marveled at the energy and patience of these insects, and going around the ant hill, we continued on.

The machete work was getting lighter. At one point, however, we ran into a dense thicket of tropical trees, and a *tapón* of fallen ones. Both Carmen and Pablo tried different directions to slash their ways out. I stayed behind Alcira. Soon there were two separate paths ahead. Alcira started down one and I let her go. As long as I was behind her, she wouldn't head back on the trail. A mule has that tendency.

Then I heard Carmen call from down the other path. I went down to see what he wanted. He said that it was impossible in this direction and he had better go and see if Pablo had found a way out. Then I thought of the mule. We ran back to see Alcira heading back on the trail and disappear into the jungle. Carmen ran off down the trial after her.

If the mule got away and maybe lost herself in the jungle, all our gear would go with it. Pablo and I waited anxiously. Fifteen minutes later Carmen returned with Alcira, still cursing her. I looked her in the face and said loudly, *"Mula!"* Alcira flicked her ears and began to munch on some leaves. Mules are incorrigible. After awhile we found a way around the *tapón* and continued on toward the Rio.

After more than two kilometers, we hadn't reached it. Pablo couldn't understand why. It seemed to me that we were heading more west than north. I checked my compass. I was right. Setting a dead-north course, we started out.

After only a few hundred yards, we reached the Rio Machaquilá. It was full and moving along at a fair speed. I could hardly believe it. We had reached our first objective. The Rio was ours!

It was still early in the afternoon. We were hot, tired and hungry, because in our anxiety to reach the Rio before dark, we hadn't eaten since morning. Pablo and I slung the hammocks, while Carmen hurriedly cleaned the *faisano* and started to cook it. Just as it was done it started to rain in huge drops; a downpour started.

We each grabbed a piece of *faisano* and our coffee and got into our hammocks. The meat was good, but I preferred the taste of the *mancolola* of the day before. After eating I dozed off. When I woke up the sun was out again. The rain had cooled the jungle and it was a beautiful day.

Our camp was forty feet from the Rio. I went over to it and started down its steep twenty-foot bank. It was thick with underbrush and I had to chop my way down, stomping steps in the muddy bank as I went. The Rio was only about fifty feet across at this point, the water low and clear. I could see the bottom and estimated that it must be only five feet deep. There were even a few sharp rocks jutting out of it. It was moving slowly at a few kilometers an hour.

That night was a sort of farewell evening. We sat around the fire talking and sipping from our bottles of *indita*. It would be farewell to Carmen and Alcira the mule. They would leave in the morning and return to Poptún while Pablo and I continued ahead by river. It was also farewell to heavy machete-swinging and moving through dense jungle. The Rio would now be our trail to the ruins. We went to bed late and in a happy *indita* mood.

I woke up during the night and found myself soaking wet from the waist up. It was raining and my hammock was leaking. I had to get out and restretch the cover piece. It took me a half hour to get a fire going. The rain stopped, and I finally managed to get my shirt dry. Pablo and Carmen were asleep but I could hear Alcira, as usual munching on leaves in the darkness.

The jungle night was full of sounds. Strange bird calls and odd cricketlike sounds constantly came out of the darkness. I could hear animals passing through the jungle; some seemed to be no more than fifty feet away. But there was little danger. There are few animals that bother man, unless he provokes them. Even a *tigre* will rarely attack, although he is a night prowler. I could even hear the river running below the camp and I guessed that the rain must have deepened it some. Listening to these sounds and looking into the smoldering embers of the fire, I almost hypnotized myself with the mystery of the night. A mosquito bite on the ear snapped me out of it. I had a last cigarette and at two in the morning went back to sleep.

Carmen was up at dawn. I could hear him talking to Alcira. Later Pablo and I got up and had Nu-V bars and coffee for breakfast. Carmen then handed me a limp-looking piece of wood. *Cambó*, he called it. It was a half inch thick and six inches long. He said he got it in the jungle that morning, and that it was the heart of a coroso palm. He said it was good to eat. I tried it and it was almost tasteless.

Later Pablo asked Carmen if he could take his rifle with us. Carmen said he needed it himself and only had five rounds left anyway. I said it didn't matter as I had my pistol and fifteen rounds of ammo. Pablo was satisfied, but I got the odd feeling that Carmen didn't think we were coming back. He had repeated several times the night before that he thought the river trip was suicide. We had been drinking, and the truth always comes out with alcohol. That morning Carmen had not mentioned his opinion of the river trip at all.

At seven o'clock Carmen had packed Alcira and was ready to leave. I gave him a letter to post for me in Poptún. It was to my parents. In it I said I would write again in ten days when I came out of the jungle. Then I paid Carmen thirty quetzales for his and Alcira's services. It included that day and the next. On the open trail we had now cut, it would only take him two days to return. I also gave him eight Nu-V bars and a pack of cigarettes.

Then I went over to say good-bye to Alcira. I patted the old mule on the neck. I would miss her. Alcira was unconcerned, munching on a handful of corn that Carmen had given her. Then Pablo and I shook Carmen's hand in turn, and said *adios*. He smiled, wished us luck and leading Alcira, disappeared into the jungle.

~~~~~~

1 · TAPÓNS AND RAPIDS

Now PABLO AND I stood alone, our backs to the Rio. Pablo went down the bank to look at our new adversary, while I took the rubber boat out of the pita bag and started to inflate it. When he returned awhile later, I had one half of the boat bulging with air. I undid the pump, closed the valve and started on the other side. Pablo said the Rio was higher than the day before and running a bit faster, due to the night's heavy rains. I continued pumping and Pablo went back to widen the path down the bank of the Rio so we could get the boat safely through.

When the boat was inflated, I carried it down to Pablo, who was waiting on the river's edge. He placed it in the water and tied it to a branch. The two-man eight-by-four-foot boat suddenly looked tiny in the water—but sturdy. It was yellow on top, and had a blue flooring. I assembled the two collapsible aluminum oars and put them inside. Then we went back to break camp.

When the hammocks were unslung and everything in order, we still had three packs—my frame pack, which weighed fifty pounds, Pablo's pack, which weighed twenty-five, and the pita bag, now down to twenty pounds, without the boat. And so at eight-thirty on the morning of November 25th, we entered the unknown waters of the Machaquilá and headed downstream.

For me the moment was one of adventurous expectation and a strange doubt, or fear. Fear of the unknown. We had no idea what lay ahead. I could see in Pablo's eyes the mood I felt, but while I had a determined confidence, I knew he had firm misgivings.

First of all, he had never been in a boat on a river, although he did know how to swim. Secondly, as did the rest of the people in the area, he considered the Machaquilá cursed— a river to avoid. Burdened with such thoughts, his was an act braver than mine. I felt a sudden pride for the man. Although his paddling was bad he was learning quickly. In the jungle he was a man of iron: tireless, brave and an expert with the machete. On the river, he was a novice. In fact, we both were. I hadn't paddled in fifteen years, but it is something one doesn't forget.

The Rio was beautiful, only fifty or sixty feet wide, rippling along gently and overhung with trees. We entered a small, choppy rapid, but soon slid through into calm water again. It was very humid, the sun was in and out among the thunderhead clouds and the temperature was in the eighties. We began to smile and talk with confidence.

About four kilometers downriver, we passed a fifteen-foot arroyo which entered the Rio on the right. Then we came upon our second rapid. Farther on, coming out of our third rapid, we ran smack into a tree across the Rio, a *tapón* which completely stopped our course. I had a cigarette and tried to figure a way through. Soon we were chopping away with our machetes, and after awhile managed to slip under it and continue.

The water was getting deeper now and muddy, the clear blue-gray fading into pale yellow and then yellow-brown. But it was more beautiful than ever against the deep tropical greens of the jungle. Pablo estimated its depth at six meters. Soon many dead stumps and sticks under the water began to appear, but they were no danger. We could see a foot or two beneath the pale waters, and our rubber boat only drew eight inches.

Birds of all sorts began to crisscross ahead on the Rio, emitting strange, shrill calls. Pablo said they were mostly *patos*, a large blue-black water fowl.

We saw some *ceiba* trees, but mostly the banks were covered with *amate* and *mahagua* trees, with an occasional *jauate* and corozo palm. The banks were covered with vines and tree branches, but even so I could see that they were low and not much higher than the Rio, possibly four or five feet.

Now and then an iguana, some five feet long, would drop out of a tree and into the water ahead of us. They are strange lizards, with the look of an ugly horned dinosaur, good eating and supposedly harmless.

Soon they were dropping every minute, some coming so close they sprayed us with water, and I was beginning to wonder if they might hit us and overturn the boat. I fired at a few with my pistol, but we only saw them in mid-air, just before they hit the water, and I missed all shots.

At midday, it started to rain like mad but, donning our ponchos, we continued paddling on through it, until we were stopped by another *tapón*. Actually, there were two trees across the river, fifty feet apart. The first one was a tremendous *ramón*, seven feet in diameter, and it looked as if it had taken the smaller one down with it when it fell. Pablo got up on the *ramón* and started to chop away at the branches in the heavy downpour. We were trying to get the boat close and lift it over. Then I saw a spot underneath it and started to hack away at a branch. Soon I was pushing and hacking my way through. I made it. Pablo got in, and at the second tree we simply got out on it and slid the boat over.

Continuing along the rain stopped, and we spotted our first *playa* (beach). It looked more like a sandbar, stretching out a way in the water. We pulled up on it (it was all mud and dead leaves), had lunch and went on.

I didn't realize until then that my sombrero was gone. I couldn't believe it. It must have gotten pushed off, as I squeezed under the *ramón* upriver. I felt bad about that but, besides sentimentality, a hat is an indispensable necessity in the jungle. Its loss amounts to a minor disaster. Besides helping to keep the rain out of your neck, it also protects you against the innumerable types of bugs and ants which fall from the trees. Later I would miss it sorely; already I felt half naked.

The river now began to widen a bit and soon turned into one snaking curve, the compass needle swinging as much as 200 degrees on some. These curves were spaced about 200 meters apart and it was almost that distance around one, so that we were continually maneuvering through them, and didn't have much time to relax on the straight stretches.

We continued at a fair pace, however, but I was not really satisfied with Pablo's paddling. One hour he did well, the next he paddled too weakly or too strongly. I could not keep up any semblance of a rhythm as I constantly had to compensate for this. We passed through a few easy rapids, then another *tapón*. With this particular one, though, came a new sight: an abandoned *ceiba* dug-out canoe lay a few inches under the water just before it. It was sixteen feet long and two feet wide.

Pablo said it was probably the canoe the men of Concomá had lost there on a fishing trip some years back. The *tapón* was a beauty, but after much difficulty we finally made it through.

Around the next curve we hit our first real rapid. It was choppy and continued beyond the next curve. I took over the paddling and tried to keep the prow dead ahead, as we bounced through the fifteen-kilometer-per-hour current. Pablo was noticeably frightened, as the spray occasionally splashed over the boat and into our faces, but I did get him to help me navigate the curve. Beyond it, the rapid ended and once more the water smoothed over and almost stopped moving. In fact, there was no noticeable current on the Rio now at all, except of course in the rapids.

The rest of the afternoon was one rapid after another, interspersed with *tapóns*. My notebook entry read like this: "Passed through three more *tapóns* within the next two kilometers. Much machete work. Finally reached a stretch of fairly fast water moving six to seven kilometers per hour, which had about nine or ten rapids. Speed fifteen to twenty kilometers per hour. Waves twelve to eighteen inches, with ten-foot rolls. Boat swamped in some. Rained heavy for an hour. Bailing. Sun out again. Took three shots at pato bird. Missed all. Couldn't get closer than one hundred feet. Should not have tried with the .32 pistol. Oh well. *La cosa es hecha* (the thing is done). Have only eight rounds of ammo left. Pablo says the pato would have been good eating. A few kilometers of dead calm water. Four P.M. Reached bad rapid with trees across it in water. Cut through. Last few kilometers had four more rapids, as bad as worst previous ones. Four fifteen, decided to camp. Found ten foot long by five foot wide playa. Moored boat and set up camp to side of playa on edge of ten foot steep bank, beautiful spot."

It *was* a beautiful spot. We had a *playa*, a high bank with a view of the Rio, and behind us were some corozo palms. The

underbrush wasn't thick, and in a few minutes we had a camp
site cleared and I started to unpack. Everything was soaked
and so were Pablo and I, but I felt good. It was the first day
down the Rio, and we were now deep in the jungle in unexplored river country. The Rio was rough going, I thought, but
not impossible. In three or four days we'd be at the ruins. On
that last thought I was wrong. Almost dead wrong.

While I was unpacking and daydreaming, Pablo had gathered some wood. There wasn't much, but the center stems of
dead corozo palms are great for starting fires. I worked on the
fire, and Pablo spread both our hammocks under his shelter
tarp. Our camp was on the right side of the Rio looking downstream, and close to the steep bank.

We opened our first can of corned beef for supper, and
began to eat and talk. Pablo said that Carmen overcharged me
for his time and mule. I said I knew it, but as I wanted him to
come I didn't say anything. I was paying double wages anyway so that Carmen and he would risk the trip. I said I knew it
was a dangerous undertaking. Pablo agreed with that. But I
was short on money, and everything else for that matter, including food and film.

I knew I had rushed into the whole affair from the start.
But if I hadn't I'd now be back in little old New York fighting
the rat race, I thought. I had no regrets. No matter how difficult the trip, it would be worth the experience. No one has
lived until they've been inside the jungle. Then I thought
about Pablo. He was a nicer chap than Carmen. Doesn't know
from anything, I thought, and he's a poor oarsman, but will-
ing.

We stripped to dry our clothes near the fire. My hands
ached with the thorns I had in them from the *tapón* branches,
but now I noticed large red spots all over my body, especially
around the stomach. I knew even mosquitoes couldn't have
managed all that through my clothing. *Arradores*, Pablo said.

He explained that they were tiny, ticklike river bugs and that the bites wouldn't begin to itch for a day or two, when the eggs they had laid under the skin began to move.

Before bed that night I looked at my notes, and made some additions. I estimated we had gone twenty-three kilometers on the Rio, and I had noted eighteen rapids and seven *tapóns*. No coming day would have as many of either, and yet it was to be our easiest day on the Rio and the most kilometers we were to travel on it in a single day. If I had known it that night, I might have had second thoughts about continuing, for it had been a very rough day. But beautiful.

If you ever ask an explorer how the jungle is he will, nine times out of ten, start with "beautiful." That is a true explorer. The man of action. The "tourist" explorer, on the other hand, talks about the dangers and discomforts first. A true explorer may mention these, but as an afterthought. He takes them for granted. It's part of the game. He knows one pays for everything in life, and to him those things are easily compensated for by the beauty and mystery of the jungle. To him, they are *part* of the beauty. If you think I mean part of the adventure, you have misunderstood: you will never really understand the jungle. And the jungle is life.

Pablo was already asleep in his hammock. I went down to the boat on the *playa,* and looked up through the trees along the Rio. The night was dark, the sky full of stars. It was one of the most peaceful and beautiful moments I can remember. The stars, tiny specks of blue and white, the beautiful silhouette of the trees, black against the Prussian-blue sky, the sound of the water running in the Rio . . . the jungle night with its strange murmur of soundless sounds, broken by the occasional eerie cry of who knows what bird or animal—a mysterious, hypnotic dream. I stood there a long time.

Back in my hammock, I dozed off to other dreams, but woke up later wet and cold. At the fire my fatigue shirt was almost dry. I put it over my khaki shirt, had a cigarette and went back to sleep. I woke again, this time from the pain in my left hand, from the cuts and spines in it. Now I was worrying about the coming day. I hoped I could paddle without pain. My feet were freezing. I rubbed them and then checked the thermometer in my pocket, and my wristwatch. It was sixty-two degrees, and two-thirty in the morning. I noticed the fire was dead, but it seemed fairly light. The moon was out. I fell asleep watching the moonbeams through the trees.

2 · CAPSIZE

I WOKE UP AT five, just as dawn was breaking, and went down to the Rio. The river had risen a foot during the night and the *playa* was gone, but the boat was safely afloat. Bracing myself on the steep muddy bank, I started to fill my canteen, but slipped and slid into the Rio, sinking into the mud and water to my waist. I returned to camp smiling at my stupidity, and woke Pablo up. He too smiled at my wet pants, but said it didn't matter much as we'd be soaked again by the next rain anyhow. (As we sat in the boat, the ponchos only kept us dry from the waist up.)

As we ate breakfast, coffee and Nu-Vs, my *arrador* bites began to itch. Pablo had been right, but they were not as bad as I had feared. My left hand was still sore from the spines, and slightly numb. I was getting used to the ache. I swabbed it with antiseptic and finished off breakfast by washing two APC tablets down with a swig of Irish whisky. Pablo had a shot, the first in his life, and said it was *muy rico* (very rich), a phrase only used when something is exceptionally good.

We broke camp and at seven-thirty re-entered the Rio. It was wild-looking and noisy again with bird calls after the quiet of the night, and soon we found it was just a continuation of the rapids of the end of the previous day.

In an hour we passed through four very bad ones, each only a hundred yards long, but with twenty-kilometer-per-hour water rushing through three- and four-foot waves over rocks. It was one swift, dangerous stretch of choppy water after another.

On the fifth rapid of the day we got swamped, so violently were we tossed about, and almost went under. Just in time we grabbed a passing tree limb and pulled over to a bank of the Rio. We had taken thirty gallons of water (the boat would hold about fifty) and spent some time bailing, with only one empty coffee can between us.

The next seven kilometers were worse than ever. We shot fifteen rapids in all, and each seemed to be faster-moving than the one before, choppier and more treacherous than the last. Pablo tried to pretend that it was great sport, occasionally smiling, but I knew he was scared as hell. I had my moments too, but the real fear and danger was not of drowning, as we were both good swimmers, but of getting our brains dashed out on a rock if we capsized in the churning current. At the least we might lose our equipment or even the boat itself, and be stranded out in that uncharted wilderness.

But I consoled myself that the rapids moved fast, and were bringing us closer and closer to the ruins. With the slowest speed of the water about eight kilometers per hour, and more than twice that in the rapids, we were averaging ten kilometers per hour. I was estimating every stretch and curve of the Rio and even jungle-wise Pablo agreed with my estimations of kilometer distances.

At this point I estimated fifteen kilometers for the day and it was only nine-thirty in the morning. I told Pablo confidently that we would be at the ruin the next day. It was a foolish statement for an unexplored Rio.

Up ahead we spotted a particularly bad-looking rapid. Pablo said maybe it was better to go around it, in the jungle. I pulled off the Rio at a dead tree along the left bank to ponder the situation.

Taking out my binoculars, I looked ahead at the rapid and discovered a ten-foot-wide clear shoot on the right side. The left side had a large fallen tree just before the rapid and over it rolled a giant wave of water. Beyond in the rapid, huge rolling choppy waves were thundering, but only on the left side. If we could navigate the right side through the shoot, beyond it the water was passable.

I untied the packs from the boat to dig into my frame pack for something, and made a near-fatal mistake. I forgot to re-tie them.

We got in the boat and paddled toward the rapid. As we approached it, I told Pablo that when we approached the shoot I'd take it through as usual. Pablo was scared stiff, his eyes glued to the churning waters ahead. He wasn't paddling hard enough and finally stopped altogether. The man of iron had turned to stone.

By now the rapid current was thrusting us ahead and we ended up sideways in midstream. Having no chance to reach the shoot, I straightened the boat out just in time to bounce over the wave which plunged over the submerged tree. On the other side the water was boiling foam, and we crashed into a half dozen five-foot waves.

On the second or third wave the front end of the boat went straight up. I threw myself forward to try to keep it from flipping, but it was too late. Pablo sat there frozen, and I saw him stiffly slip into the water just before the whole thing came down on me.

A pack hit me on the head and I went straight down. Half unconscious, I reached the surface and saw the boat upside down, twenty feet away and going downstream fast. I swam furiously toward it, almost in panic. Suddenly a sobering thought struck me. Where was Pablo?

I continued toward the boat, but something was holding me back. When I reached it, I was ready to go down. I grabbed desperately for the tow rope around it. I made it, then looked back for Pablo. He was nowhere in sight. I felt a dull ache in my heart and although the water was cold a hot flush came over me, then a terrible series of realizations. Pablo had drowned or struck his head on a rock. Pablo was dead! I was alone. All the packs were gone. No equipment. No food. Even our pistol belts, which we took off in the boat for paddling and tossed recklessly on its floor, were gone.

This last thought was as shocking as any. I had heard that a man can lose everything in the jungle and still survive—everything, that is, except one thing: his machete! And mine was on my pistol belt, which was now somewhere at the bottom of the Rio.

I suddenly saw the shore going by fast and it snapped me back to reality and action. Looking downstream, I saw a dead tree sticking out along the river bank into the Rio. I struck out for it, pulling the boat, but it was hard going. It looked as if I wouldn't make it, and beyond was a curve and maybe another rapid. I refused to abandon the boat and kept struggling toward the dead-tree side of the Rio, the right. Then it came to me what had been pulling me down: my rubber boots. One had slipped off. I kicked the other loose and barely grabbed a limb of the dead tree as I drifted by.

Then a stroke of luck. I saw Pablo's pack up against the trunk of the tree. I managed to make my way to it and grab it. Reaching the bank, I slumped down in exhaustion and near shock. Pablo was still not to be seen. Maddening visions of tracking back along the Rio, nights in the jungle without a hammock, and of being lost deep in the jungle flashed through my brain in a dizzying sequence. My compass was gone, in a pouch on my pistol belt. My pistol, I thought, clutching inside my shirt. I had it! My only defense and hunting weapon.

Thinking Pablo dead, I hadn't bothered to call out to him. Now I tried, but my voice was weak. I was beat and dejected. I sat, unthinking, and my fear faded into an unaware calm. I refused to think of my situation, even to move.

Then I saw a movement along my side of the Rio about 200 feet upstream toward the rapid. A figure stood erect. It was Pablo! Excitedly I called out as loud as I could and waved. He saw me and waved back. He held up something and I could see it was my frame pack. I was happy as hell to see Pablo, and he had also saved a pack!

Pulling the boat behind me, I jumped chest-deep in the water and started to wade over to him. I had to swim a way but finally I reached him. We were both yelling and laughing like two kids. Then we clasped hands. The initial shock of the capsize was over.

I tied up the boat and we made our way around the fallen tree in the water. Behind it was a beautiful sandy beach, thirty feet long and ten wide, with plenty of dry wood. A beautiful spot to capsize, I thought. The rapid ended another hundred feet upriver and it was churning like mad, sending a steady low roar through the jungle. The sun came out and glistened across the turbulent Rio and it felt good to be alive.

I asked Pablo what had happened. He said he had grabbed both oars just after he had hit the water. Then he saw my pack, and going after it, slammed up against a rock. His nose and forehead had cuts, but they were not too bad. He said they were still numb. Almost drowning, but without dropping oars or pack, he had made it to shore and there dozed off into unconsciousness.

I told him he was a brave man. He liked that. I on the other hand had almost panicked. We had saved both oars, my frame pack and Pablo's bag. The pita bag was lost. We started to check what was lost and what we still had. I made a list.

Food left: 48 Nu-V bars
Two cans corned beef
One 8-ounce box Bolton biscuits
Two small cans pemmican
Two cans of sardines
One small can Spam. And one woodsmen's emergency kit (containing one can pemmican, two tropical chocolate bars, matches and small emergency compass).

As to what we lost, it was disastrous, beginning with *both* machetes and two hunting knives. Now all we had to replace these was my Swiss army knife. I had lost my compass, but Pablo still had his. Both our leather boots were lost in the pita bag, together with the shelter tarp, both flashlights, our only two cans of powdered milk and thirty Nu-V bars. My still camera and my binoculars were ruined. I took the lenses apart on the movie camera and cleaned them, while Pablo built a fire and started to dry things. Most of my movie film was wet. My sketch pads were all gone in the pita bag. Luckily my notebook, inside my shirt and in a plastic bag, was safe and fairly dry.

I reviewed the situation. No machetes, no shoes, and only eight or nine days' food supply left, if we stretched it out. That was it in a nutshell. I discussed it with Pablo while I put antiseptic on his face cuts. He was for turning back. I was, naturally, for going on to the ruins. I explained my point.

We were now sixty trail kilometers, plus forty more by river, from Poptún. Without machetes the jungle was impenetrable, not to mention unknown, between here and Poptún.

We would have to follow the Rio to our point of entry, and then find the trail we cut. Besides, I said, how can we even follow the river bank through the jungles without machetes?

Pablo began to insist we'd be in Poptún in five or six days. He was going back. Alone? I asked. Yes, he said. Would I give him the jackknife? I said I would and half of the food. He asked if I were really going down the Rio alone. I said definitely that I was. And I meant it. I said we couldn't be more than forty river kilometers from the ruin, and that was a two-day trip. From there, after the one day at the ruin, four more days on the Rio to the Rio Pasion and three more to Sayaxche. A total of ten days, I said.

Pablo thought awhile. He could see I meant to go on, with or without him. I knew he didn't fancy the return to Poptún alone.

"If you go alone down that Rio," he said seriously, "you will die."

"Maybe," I said, "but are you sure you'll reach Poptún alone?"

He thought about that one. I told Pablo that if we went to the ruins, it would be safer for both of us. He had to concede the point, but he still hesitated about going with me.

We started to work on our gear again, and continued drying things for a long time. My watch was battered, as I had scraped it along a rock in the rapids. The crystal was scratched and the grooves full of mud. I couldn't see the hands. Cleaning it off with lighter fluid, I saw it was almost two o'clock in the afternoon. We had a few Nu-V bars and started talking again about where we'd go from here.

Pablo said that without machetes and shoes, to go deeper into the jungle was suicide. I said we'd be mostly on the river, before and after the ruin, and that as far as shoes went we could wrap cloth around our feet. After that we could cut up Pablo's *chalveque* bag and fashion sandals from it. (This bag he still had slung across his chest, resting on his right hip. Many Guatamalens carry one and it is the size of an average sling purse.) Pablo thought this was a good idea, but being an old *chiclero* he was lost without his machete.

Finally everything was fairly dry. We repacked our bags and went to the boat.

"Which way are you going, Pablo?" I said, pointing at the Rio, "*Arriba o abajo?*" (Up or down?).

Pablo smiled. "*Va bien,*" he said, "*con usted*" (OK, with you), and we got into the boat and started downstream.

I looked back at the rapid and the churning waters which had cost us so much in equipment, and very nearly our lives. I couldn't hate it. It was part of the jungle, wild and untamed. A jungle which was neither hostile nor friendly, but just was.

In this uncompromising world, we were the intruders, and we would have to take our chances like men and not hate an entity which existed without human considerations. In the jungle there is only one law. No law. Survival of the strong. Conquer or be conquered. But there is no malice. The jungle is nature. Unplanned, untamed and unaware, where justice has no conception. Justice is a human invention, intended to tame, order and give meaning to something which is beyond such strivings. Against nature, man is doomed to lose, but for awhile he can still hope to exist within it.

Maybe it was this desire to go back into time and live within nature for a while as our ancestors had, instead of fighting it, that had brought me to this last bit of an untouched world called a jungle. I only knew that whatever else it might be, it was beautiful. And free.

3 · CASCADES:
Life or Death on the Rio

PABLO AND I paddled around the next bend of the Rio and could see that there were no rapids in sight. The straight stretches were getting longer, about 300 yards.

Then I saw Pablo cock his ear. He told me to stop paddling. He listened and announced a large *rápido* (rapid) ahead, maybe a *cascada* (waterfall), he said with speculation. I heard it now, and as we approached the curve it grew louder and louder, until rounding the bend of the Rio it was a roar, and we came upon a tremendous network of rapids and cascades, tumbling down in huge torrents of water over an irregular series of steps and passages. It was a veritable watery hell. We headed straight for the nearest bank (it was the right), paddling furiously, the current sucking us ahead faster and faster, until barely thirty feet before the first cascade, full of awe and fear, we grabbed on to some limbs along the bank and managed to come to a stop. It had been close, and now we sorely missed our lost machetes.

The bushes and trees ranged out into the Rio at least ten feet. It was impossible to get through the thick tangle to the shore, which we could hardly see. We started to make our way bush by bush, limb by limb, along the bank until we had reached the roaring edge of the first plunging precipice.

Moving along treetrunks and rocks which cut our shoeless feet (we wore only socks), we managed to lower ourselves and the boat down the first of these steplike cascades. Near the bank they were only flowing moderately compared to the tumbling, roaring confusion that was the center of the Rio.

The complex of cascades went around the next curve and finally, after a tremendous hour-long effort, we descended the final one, some 250 yards downstream. Near exhaustion, we rested awhile, each had a Nu-V bar; then we got into the boat and started out again.

As the roar of the cascades behind us faded, we could already hear another ahead. Reaching it, we saw it was bad, but not like the last one. It fell in two five-foot cascades; interspersed between them, and beyond the second one, were rocks and rapids, tossing large waves.

Again we made our way along the shore, but this time it was much easier and the whole thing amounted to less than 150 yards.

Within the next kilometer we passed through two more cascades—or, I should say, struggled our way around them. Pablo was complaining about his lost machete, and I about my aching hands and feet, which besides being cut had accumulated a new crop of *espinas* (spines or thorns).

As we continued downriver the sun kept sinking lower ahead of us until finally it was in our eyes, and reflecting blindingly off the water. I put on my sunglasses so I could see better and not run into another cascade and topple over it. It looked clear. I checked the time. Four P.M. Then it started to rain, hard. In a minute, before we could get to our ponchos, we were soaking wet.

It was already late so we decided we'd had enough for one day. We picked out a spot, pulled off the Rio and cut inland a hundred feet before we found a good campsite.

The site we now needed had to have two trees, ten or twelve feet apart, plus another tree four or five feet to the side of one of them. Without his shelter tarp, Pablo now had to build a *champa* (a palm-branch lean-to) every night. His hammock had no cover, and mine was not as waterproof as it could have been. Both hammocks would have to be slung under it, thus the need for the third tree.

I was amazed at how fast Pablo built his *champa*. He would cut a small tree, trim the limbs, and get a fifteen-foot pole out of it. Then, with one-eighth-inch-thick *bejucos* (vines), which hung down everywhere and which he ripped from the treetops with one great yank, he started.

With the vines he tied the pole between two trees about five feet off the ground. Then he'd cut twenty or thirty corozo or guano fronds, varying from twelve to fifteen feet in length, and lean them across the pole between the trees, and the thing was done. For a *champa*, one of course needs corozo or guano palms nearby, so we had to choose our campsites accordingly, and also find the three strategically placed trees.

When the corozo or guano trees were nearby, it took Pablo only fifteen minutes to build one. I would find firewood, and while I started to sling the hammocks under Pablo's completed *champa*, he would start the fire going. I wasn't bad, but I was no match for old Pablo in quick fire-starting.

That night, being tired, we barely set up camp and got the fire started before darkness fell at five-thirty. By six o'clock it was pitch-black and we didn't stray outside our *champa* area.

Tigres and snakes are on the prowl in full force during the dark hours of the jungle. Snakes are unpredictable but usually not dangerous, unless you step on one or it falls on you from a tree limb. At night both these hazards are multiplied. As for the *tigre*, he is not likely to attack a man in broad daylight, but if surprised at night he may do so. The best way to avoid both dangers at night is to stay close to the fire or in your hammock.

That evening we again started to dry some things by the fire. I was especially worried about my movie film. It was all I had left to record anything graphically about the trip. The still camera was gone, along with my sketch pads. Only the movie

camera remained, and I still had my eight-by-six-inch notebook inside my shirt.

Going through his bag, Pablo discovered a hunting knife
with a six-inch blade that I had given him. Nothing could have
made us happier at this point, except a machete—or possibly a
helicopter to carry us to the ruins. We were soaked and exhausted, and the trip ahead looked like cascades and rapids all
the way.

But now we had an edge: a good sturdy six-inch cutting
edge to hack our way through the jungle. Compared to the
Swiss army knife I had, it was almost like finding a machete.

When Pablo also found his flashlight, I declared a holiday
and pulled out the Irish whisky. We sat around the fire smoking some of the cigarettes we had dried, and taking an occasional pull on the bottle. Now and then Pablo would talk
about the Rio Torcido and how the whole trip looked cursed.
I told him that in a few days we'd reach the ruins and in less
than a week the Rio Pasion. He said I was probably right, and
we got into our hammocks in a relaxed mood. Between our
exhaustion and the whisky we had no trouble getting to sleep,
even though we were both half wet.

The next day after we broke camp and before we started
on the Rio again, I checked my map to see if I could get an
accurate estimate of our position on the Machaquilá. I was
using the latest and best map of the area, the *Mapa Preliminar
de la Republica de Guatemala,* dated 1959 and with a scale of
1:750,000 (nineteen kilometers or twelve miles to the inch).
Though it was the best available map and a good one, it was
not accurate in respect to the Machaquilá. For one thing, it
was a little too small for strict accuracy. Then the Machaquilá
was called the Santa Amelia, while another river below it was
named the Machaquilá. The curves of the Rio were not correct, as it had never been navigated. I think the curvatures of
the river were simply made up—at best only approximations.

As for estimating our position on this map, it could only be an educated guess.

From my notes I began to draw a rough sketch of the Rio as it lay so far. I had made numerous compass checks along the Rio, and now using Pablo's compass I continued making frequent checks as we continued downriver.

One of the first things I noticed when we stepped into the boat that morning was that it had lost air. This was alarming, for the air pump had been lost in the capsize. I had no idea whether I could inflate it by mouth—that is, whether I could put more air in it than it now had (it was now very low). It was beginning to buckle in the center and lay much lower in the water. Pablo was even more worried than I was, and again began talking about turning back. In spite of everything, I insisted that things weren't *that* bad and that even the river was much better than yesterday.

It was true. In a whole kilometer we hadn't had one cascade or rapid. Pablo kept on talking of turning back, so to calm him down I told a lie. I said I was sure I could inflate the boat by mouth, and furthermore that if he still didn't trust the boat, we would now only camp on the left side of the Rio at night. The ruin was on that side. If the boat failed us, I said, we could still walk to the ruins.

When I said that, he was quiet for awhile, but then began to lament the fact that he had no machete to cut his way to the ruin. He had me there, but I retorted that the knife with the six-inch blade would get us there. He said it might but it was no machete. Just as I mentioned how good the Rio was again, with no cascades, we heard a familiar hum ahead of us. Another cascade.

When we reached it, we saw at once that it would take us an hour to get through. It did. But worse was to come. Around the next curve was another, and we could see that a hundred yards beyond it was another. I had been noting them in my book. This last one was the sixth cascade so far, and it didn't include all the rapids we had been through.

The day turned out to be a nightmare. Within the next kilometer we went around three more cascades, now always on the left-hand side. They were not steep—some were only three or four feet high—but one was a double one and this was as bad as two. Pablo was working hard on these stretches, clinging to the bank and sometimes, in water up to his chest, pulling the boat along the shore. I was letting him eat four or five Nu-V bars a day now, to help him keep up his strength. I settled for two.

At the cascades I would go along the shore through the jungle, and it was rough. The mosquitoes ate me alive, even though I had sprayed myself, the spines and thorns tore my clothes and stuck into my hands and the vines entangled me and grabbed at my ankles as I tried to cut my way through with only my Swiss army jackknife.

My feet were now full of spines, and at one point we had to stop and wrap some pita cloth from my frame pack around them. Still the spines came through. Pablo said he would cut his leather chalveque bag and make sandals, but I told him to save it until we reached the ruin.

Early in the afternoon we reached our tenth cascade. Three hundred more yards and the eleventh, 250 more and the twelfth, and here, lowering the boat down a steep cascade, it swamped and almost sank. It was full to the brim with about fifty gallons and our packs were again soaked. Having lost our bailing can, all we had now was the canteen and our hands to do the job. There was no place to turn the boat over as the shore was a continual tangle of bushes and many of them were spines. We couldn't turn it over in the water as I wouldn't chance losing the packs, tied on or not. We did tilt it a bit, but still it took a lot of bailing to get it fairly dry inside.

We continued on down the Rio, coming upon cascade

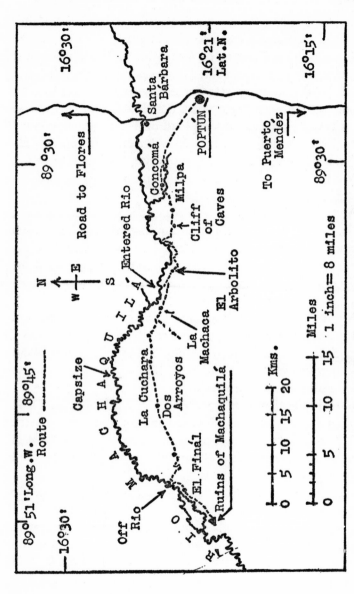

Area of jungle expedition showing author's route

after cascade. In less than a kilometer we circumvented numbers thirteen, fourteen and fifteen. After going around the fifteenth, we saw that the next one was only 300 yards downstream. We'd had enough. Besides, it was late and time to build our *champa* for the night, and we felt starved and exhausted. In all the turmoil, fighting our way around the cascades, we had forgotten to eat lunch.

Pablo had estimated a five-day trip from Poptún to the ruins and I had put it at six days. It was now the end of our seventh day, and if things kept up as they had this last day, it was sure to take at least another two. Some of our food supply had been lost. We were in a desperate struggle against time and the river. Already behind our schedule, uncertain of the Rio and with our lives hanging in the balance, the jungle around us began to assume the form of a waiting vulture in my mind, and I had the feeling that someone or something was looking at us from its depths.

We made camp quickly and began hurriedly to eat our dwindling rations, making up for the missing lunch. I felt as if I was eating my life away, but no pun was intended at the time. The situation was dead serious.

When we had finished eating it was already dark and we built a large fire. In the jungle a fire has many uses, but it is also a comforting companion. We dried some things and then I began to doctor my wounds. My hands were full of cuts, bruises and spines. My left one alone had four one-inch rips, fairly deep. My body was full of the large red itchy *arrador* bites, and my feet were an aching pair of pin cushions, imbedded with spine points. I swabbed everything with Listerine and managed to squeeze out a few spins here and there, but most would have to fester and be squeezed out later. They were just too deep for me to get at then.

I noticed that Pablo had used guano palm fronds to make the *champa* that night. I asked him if they were as good as corozo fronds. He said they were better, because the rain didn't penetrate them as easily and they lasted longer. Pablo said that when a roof was thatched with them it lasted twenty-five years, whereas corozo thatching had to be replaced every five years. Both of us were very tired and without bothering to dry any more clothing, we went to bed.

Later I woke up freezing. My fatigue jacket was wet and my feet were like ice. I got the fire going again and dried the jacket a little, also my socks. Back to sleep. But I woke up again at four A.M. The thermometer had broken the day before, but I knew the temperature was no higher than sixty degrees. I was so cold I couldn't get back to sleep, and for awhile I lay in my hammock watching the moon through the trees to the east. Then I got up, rebuilt the fire and started to dry my clothes. Next I went through all my gear, throwing away anything that wasn't absolutely necessary.

We hadn't tried yet to inflate the boat by mouth, and I wasn't even sure I could. We needed a light boat if we were to continue. In any case it was a dread, because the ruins were only halfway between Poptún and the Rio Pasion, down the Machqauilá. If I couldn't get more air into the boat, we might make the ruins, but never the Pasion.

Pablo got up as dawn broke, and when it was light enough we went to the Rio, cleared a spot along the bank and carried the boat ashore. It looked worse than ever.

Pablo had gotten up in a negative mood and said that if I couldn't inflate the boat any more than it was we'd have to try to return to Poptún.

Opening a valve, I began to blow as hard as I could. Soon Pablo began to shout and point excitedly at the boat. "*Mira, mira! Esta bien, esta bien!*" (Look, it's good!) I was surprised at how easily it inflated. I couldn't get it as hard as the pump did, but it was much better than before. Pablo was all smiles.

We had some of the Irish whisky and the world looked bright again.

Breaking camp, we floated down to the sixteenth cascade and went around it along the shore. It was a double one, with fifty feet between the falls, each one being about five feet high. Most of the cataracts up to now had only been three to four feet high. The highest had been the first one, a series of cascading rapids with a total drop of not less than thirty feet. Two hundred yards ahead lay the next one.

Getting into the boat to paddle down to it, I grabbed a tree without looking at it. It was a *baiál* tree with three-inch spines on it; I took seven in my right hand, which looked like a pin cushion before I pulled them out.

The seventeenth cascade was only two feet high, so we got out, lowered the boat over it, and continued. The Rio now had an occasional spot in it about 150 feet wide, but mostly it averaged ninety, and some spots still narrowed down to sixty feet across. Along the shores I had been picking up two- to three-inch conchlike snail shells, colored white-and-brown, which were long and thin rather than round. Some still had the snails inside, but most of them were empty.

The next two kilometers brought a series of seven cascades some 400 feet apart. We had to circumvent most of them, but on a few we lowered the boat and, jumping in the water after it, went on. The struggle with the Rio was becoming so strenuous and time-consuming, it would have seemed ridiculous if our situation had been less dangerous. Getting wet in the Rio didn't matter any more. Hands and feet full of spines and cuts didn't matter. Mosquites became ignored pests, and aching bones and muscles were forgotten in our frenzied determination to make time on the Rio.

The river now began to assume the proportions of a living organism that consciously impeded our passage. Pablo's favorite phrase now became *Que rio torcido!* (What a cursed river!) and as the difficulties continued I could see his frustration and fear mounting. The Rio was one never-ending watery hell, and I began to think that it was cursed myself.

Still, we were putting forth a gallant effort. It was the two of us against that beautiful, untamed, unexplored Rio. And I meant to win. Through it all I had remained confident, and I could still see the beauty of the river, of the jungle, and even of our struggle. The twenty-second cascade, for instance, was something to see.

The Rio widened to a full hundred meters, and there were two islands, a small one and beyond it a larger one. The second island was about 100 feet long by half as much wide. The small one had a cascade at each end leading to the left bank. Another one started from its middle and went to the opposite shore, some 200 feet to the right. We landed on the small island and after much difficulty waded and swam to the second one. I lost my homemade sandals in the bargain.

The larger island was a tiny pearl in our ell. We rested there for half an hour. Pablo pointed out some red-bark *jiote* trees across the Rio, tall slashes of Indian red against the green jungle. They were the first and last trees of this kind we saw.

On the island itself he showed me a strange-looking plant. It was low, but had two-foot-long leaves on it, which he called *pata de vaca* (cow's foot). The ends of the long, glossy leaves branched out into two points, and Pablo said they were often used to wrap wet chicle balls in. On the island there were also some rare *cojóñ* trees, which had large green, eight-inch-long double nuts attached to its branches. The insides of these nuts were white and orange, and Pablo said a glue could be made from the pulp by boiling it. The island had one cascade on the left and three on the right. Going to the tip of the island, we managed to bypass all but one of these.

The next three cascades were all within a stretch of half a

kilometer and interspersed with small islands, their edges teeming with thorny and impenetrable bushes. The first two cascades were both doubles, and the third was a triple-tiered monster. The whole Rio was a maze of cascades, rapidslike water and specks of islands with bushes. It was hard to navigate or even to see ahead in this dangerous stretch.

It hadn't rained in over a day and the sun was merciless. I had broken my sunglasses the day before, and was dizzy from the glare off the water. My hatless head was spinning. Still we forged ahead. My feet were now cut badly and bleeding. On my insistence, Pablo fashioned a new pair of sandals from guano leaves. He said *majagua* bark would be better, but there were none of these trees in the area.

As we went on, it struck me that the Rio didn't have as many curves in it. They were now usually as much as 400 yards apart. We went on, fighting our way through cascades, one after another: twenty-six . . . twenty-seven . . . twenty-eight . . . twenty-nine. The last two were doubles. We were both ready to quit for the day when we had a break. We went along a half-kilometer stretch with no cascades. Then came the inevitable roar, but upon turning the curve we saw no cascade. Still, the roar went on, getting louder. . . .

Around the next curve we saw it. It was steaming twenty feet above its crest and before it lay a smaller cascade, which turned out to be only two feet high. We got off on the right bank, knowing we would have to portage around this one.

Unloading the boat, Pablo began to hack his way through the jungle with the hunting knife, and I helped as best I could with my jackknife. After a half hour we managed to cut and push our way through to a point some 200 feet below the cascade. The packs were no particular problem, even though in our weakness they seemed heavier than ever, but the boat was. We had to pamper it through the jungle so we wouldn't puncture it on the many spiny trees.

From our spot on the bank of the Rio we now saw that the cascade was, in fact, a waterfall, twenty feet high and extending across the width of the Rio, which had widened at this point to 250 feet. It was tremendously impressive! The center of the fall fell back in a bow effect and in the water below it was a small island, a tropical-treed beauty.

Across the Rio the jungle was tall, dark and mysterious, and the loud roar of the waterfall magnified the indescribably wild and beautiful look of the whole scene. One of nature's magnificent moods, a symphony of sight and sound.

We loaded the boat and got in, letting the current carry us ahead. Even Pablo, who was not impressed by much in the jungle, stared back in silence as we drifted off down the Rio. The spectacle had calmed our mood and made us pensive. The exhaustion and pain of the day seemed to fade. Three hundred yards ahead lay the next cascade, and it was almost four o'clock. As if to add to the spirit of the moment, we spotted our first *playa* in three days on the left bank, a hundred yards below the waterfall, and paddling across to it, beached the boat. In the jungle behind it was a small grove of corozo palms, sprouting their long fronds among the trees like giant green peacock feathers. It was the most beautiful camp site we were to find on the Rio.

Pablo built the corozo *champa* while I started a fire. We finished slinging our hammocks just as the usual late-afternoon rain began. For almost an hour it rained so hard we couldn't see the trees on the opposite side of the Rio, less than a hundred yards away; then the deluge subsided and it became an only normally heavy rainfall. The only reasonably dry spot was in our hammocks under the *champa*. I took some notes for awhile, but being tired and with the sound of the rain falling through the jungle around us, I fell into a lethargic sleep.

When I woke up it was dark. The rain had stopped but the echoing roar of the waterfall above us on the Rio had replaced

View of Zápotec ruin of Yagúl, near Oaxaca, Mexico

Street scene, Poptún

Author on hill of Poptún, with town below

Author with Jorge Sagrero and family, before Jorge's house in Tehuántepec

The Wiegand family of Quezaltenango: from left, Señora Célia, Argentina, Felipe, Hilda; and author

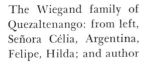

Author with Rafael Valles at top of pyramid of Poptún

Pablo, Carmen, Alcira the mule and author ready to leave Poptún on the illfated jungle trip

Rafael posing on horse, tree-engulfed ruin of Poptún rising in background

Pablo leading Alcira
across shallow ford on Rio
Concomá

Author, Pablo and Carmen at *milpa ranchera,*
second day

Author, Pablo and Carmen at entrance to cave of
spiders

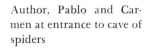

Carmen takes the lead in
dense jungle

Author inspects dry-river-
bed section of Río Macha-
quilá; Carmen in back-
ground

One of the many *tapóns*
(fallen trees) across the
Machaquilá

Rainy day on the Macha-
quilá

Numerous treetrunks in
the water, like these, finally punctured our rub-
ber boat

Author pauses to take notes in a cove of the Machaquilá

This waterfall, 20 feet high, spanned river and could be heard a mile upstream

Sacrificial altar, ruins of Machaquilá

Air view of Rio Macha-
quilá

The still weary author in
Quezaltenango, a few days
after his escape from the
jungle

it. Pablo was squatting by the fire, and I went over and joined him. His back was aching, so I rubbed it with Ben-Gay and then did the same to my arthritis-paining knees. We ate something and Pablo went off to his hammock. I dried a few things, but the wood was so wet I couldn't get a good fire going. I doctored my aching hands and feet and then went to bed myself.

I woke up at midnight, cold and shivering. I was getting used to these chilled awakenings, but tried to start the fire and warm up a bit anyway. The wet wood wouldn't catch, but I stubbornly kept trying. After an hour I gave up and went over to the Rio, only twenty feet away. The playa looked wider than when we landed. The Rio had dropped a little during the night and I couldn't understand it after the heavy rain we'd had.

I was used to it by then, but standing there I suddenly realized how really loud the waterfall was, and how it filled the surrounding jungle with its roar. I stepped out on the *playa* and looked upriver.

The sky was full of stars and a half moon made the falls a dim white blur across the Rio, giving it a ghostly beauty. It seemed paradox that such a penetrating sound was coming from that pale vision. I drifted off into a semi-hypnotic trance. I had to close my eyes and shake my head to break it.

I began to think of the past few days on the river with Pablo. If I had come down alone, I knew I should have been dead by now. I also knew that if the cascades continued as they had, we might both die in this beautiful but unrelenting jungle. We had passed through fifteen cascades the day before, and only gained six kilometers on the Rio. At that rate I estimated another four or five days to the ruins. I was so beat and bruised and aching that the figures didn't seem to impress me, even though I was aware that we were in a deadly situation.

In the jungle, which has two faces, one is always torn between mysticism and reality. On the one hand it is beautiful, mystical, abstract—a dream; on the other it is a tangle of living, dying plants and animals, locked in never-ending combat. It is unpredictable, merciless, the realest reality—the tropical growth, the rivers, the animals, insects, mud, rain, vines, spines and all its myriad discomforts and dangers.

In the end you learn one thing from the jungle: that mystical wanderings are fine and beautiful experiences, but that if one doesn't place them within a context of reality, one is doomed to fail. Life is real, concrete, and the jungle is life. No amount of mental hocus-pocus can deny it. It can be ignored, but not thought away; to ignore life is to die. The mystic who ignores reality is really a dead man.

With these thoughts I returned to my hammock and tried to "think away" my aching body so I could get back to sleep. Physical exhaustion finally did the trick.

At dawn I woke up chilled, but I soon forgot my discomfort as I looked out on the Rio in the half light. For a half hour I lay in my hammock watching the mist curling off it, the sky turning from indigo to light blue, the silhouettes of the trees taking form as the familiar leafy vegetation I knew so well.

I woke up Pablo, and lighting the fire we began to warm our chilly bones. After we ate, Pablo made new sandals for me, out of the last piece of pita cloth we had left. I went to the Rio and it seemed high again. I began to wonder if my walk to it the night before had been a dream. I noticed that the boat had lost almost no air during the night, but I had to empty the rainwater out of it.

Checking my gear, I saw I had only two fifty-foot magazines left of my sixteen-millimeter film. They ran about two and a half minutes each, or ten average pans. I decided to use the first one as a still-camera roll, on single frame, and shoot the end of it at the ruins. That would leave the second one for subsequent eventualities.

Pablo had finished my sandals and I tied them to my spine-punctured feet. We broke camp and entered the Rio, taking a last look back at the beauty of the waterfall, as we headed for the thirty-first cascade, just ahead. The cascade narrowed to thirty feet at this one, but there was a land bridge out to it, giving a laguna-like appearance. It was ten feet high, a small waterfall. We made our way across the bushy peninsula and could hear the roar of the thirty-second cascade around the next curve.

As we approached it the scene was almost a duplicate of the last cascade; land bridge, laguna, with the river flowing through on the left. We could tell from the din it was making that it was higher than the last one.

Pulling up next to it on the end of the land bridge, which was again bushy and ten feet across, I took a good look at it. It was the highest waterfall yet, and turned out to be the highest we were to encounter on the Rio. It was only thirty-five feet across but fell over thirty feet, in a thundering cascade, to the Rio below. We soon found that the land bridge fell off into a sharp cliff and beyond lay a small tree-shadowed bay.

Unloading the boat, we portaged it and the packs across, and down it to a huge slab-rock which portruded into the water of the tiny bay. It was shady and cool on the rock, and we sat there awhile to look at the bay and the fall and have a cigarette.

It was an idyllically lovely scene, with the trees hanging over the shadowed waters and the roaring white of the fall on the other side. A perfect spot to camp for a few days and enjoy nature, if we had the time. But we didn't.

Loading the boat, we paddled across the bay and into the Rio again. I can still remember the secluded beauty of the scene, and the thunder of the waterfall.

In the sky we spotted our first *zopilote* (vulture), and the last we were to see in the jungle. A lone sentinel, black against the blue sky, with outstretched wings he slowly circled, then banked off across the trees. I wondered what this king of the skies was doing way out there. So did Pablo.

Ahead lay the next cascade, and again its surroundings were similar to the last two, except it was only six feet high. The thirty-fifth was 300 yards downstream and gave us a terrible beating. It was a double drop with tiny isles, and it appeared impossible to get either through or around. The shore bushes thrust out into the water, bedecked with spines. Navigating the right bank trying to find a way through, suddenly from the bushes above we were showered by ants, half-inch black monsters.

We both took several bites on our faces and necks and tried to escape. As we did, I grabbed a bush with a bee's nest in it and a swarm of them attacked us. Pablo got it under the left eye and I took one right through the bushy hair on my scalp. We bolted out of the boat in a tangle of vines and limbs in a desperate effort to elude them. But we couldn't: it was a solid wall of growth. I took several spines in my hands, feet and legs and decided the boat was better.

Turning, I saw it was covered with gray-white "ants." Pablo saw them too. "*Garapatos!*" (Ticks!) he yelled. They were falling from bushes, and one got me in the neck. Pablo quickly got it out with a cigarette and we began to cut a trail inland.

Again we unloaded the boat and went through the struggle of a 200-yard portage through a hostile jungle area, full of vines, swamps and spine-covered bushes. When we finally emerged on the edge of the Rio below the cascade, we saw that the second drop was really a waterfall, over ten feet high and 150 feet across. I had to admit the damn thing was beautiful!

Again we loaded the boat and started out on the Rio. The next three cascades were a series, each one separated from the next by a hundred yards. The thirty-sixth was a double, but we found a water shoot and carried the boat through. On the thirty-seventh the Rio split. We took the left fork, the right being blocked by a *tapón*.

The thirty-eighth was another bad one. Again we had to portage a hundred yards around it through thick underbrush. We waded through fords, climbed over and under fallen trees; how we ever made it I'll never know. It looked impossible. What was even stranger is how we got the boat through without puncturing it, but we did.

The madness of it all was beginning to take its toll on us, physically and mentally. Pablo was completely disgusted. He had a tantrum and started shouting—we'd come upon eight cascades in the last two kilometers, and he for one was quitting! I could go on, but I was *loco*, crazy, and was going to die, and he was not, he didn't want to die; in any case he was turning back now!

I knew I had to say or do something to try to change his mind. All I could say, though, was that things just couldn't stay this bad, they were sure to get better. Pablo didn't seem to be listening; he was sitting down sulking.

I opened a can of sardines and handed it to him with a Nu-V bar. He started to eat without a word. I sat next to him, pulled my notebook out of my shirt and began to write. Pablo said I *must* be loco, writing at a time like this! My notebook entry on the incident reads as follows:

I'm not disgusted, maybe I should be, but I take things as they come. Maybe I'm crazy, but what the hell, I'm going to a ruin and damn it, I'm not worrying about how difficult it is. The thing is to get there. Christ we can't go back anyway and I wouldn't if I could.

After eating and resting for awhile, Pablo seemed in a less

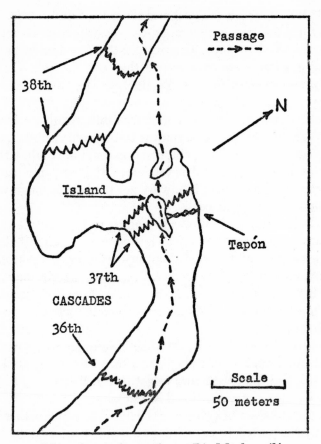

Map of typical cascades on Rio Machaquilá

hostile mood. Without a word he loaded the packs into the boat and tied them down. We got in and paddled away in silence.

We went several hundred yards with no rapids and Pablo seemed to be taking new courage. But downstream a half kilometer we heard the next one. It was only five feet high, so we threw the boat over, jumped in after it and continued on.

The next one was another kilometer ahead, and I told Pablo it was a good sign, maybe we'd soon be at the ruins. Actually I had no idea, of course, but Pablo seemed to feel better about it.

On the fortieth we dragged the boat over a narrow land bridge, thick with thorny bushes, lowered it and got in. Again we went almost a kilometer before we reached the next cascade. It was rough, and another hundred yards beyond it lay the forty-second. On both of these we had to empty the boat and portage across a land bridge. The cascade to the left of the second one was a beautiful thing, churning and shooting down in three steps, altogether about fifty-five feet long. It was thirty feet wide and the total drop must have been twenty feet.

We continued on another kilometer without the sight or sound of a cascade. Pablo was now in a much better mood and I even got him to smile. The Rio was narrower that day than it had been, averaging sixty to seventy-five feet. It was getting more tropical. Pablo pointed to the thin white trunks of trees that began to appear and said they were *guarumbo* palms. They were very tall and rose to the top of the jungle level, branching out into small topped palms. They looked like giant flowers on long white stems.

Farther down we reached the forty-third cascade, where we had to portage and go along its edge for 150 difficult meters. Below it was a rapid which we decided to go through. There was a *tapón* across it but the tree was high enough off the water to sneak under.

As we passed under it, we saw a second, unseen tree right behind it. The speed of the rapids slammed us right into it, and as it was too low to go under, we almost capsized. Groping our way along its limbs was not easy in the swift current, but we finally found the highest section of it and managed to push ourselves beneath it.

Down below, the rapid ended abruptly; we drifted into calmer water, and finally had to start paddling again. It was a magnificent spot. The trees were tall and vine-covered, with an occasional beautiful corozo palm thrusting its majestic crown of fronds up high into the tangled jungle. It was quiet, except for the sound of birds calling, their shrill and sometimes squawkish cries echoing across the calm water.

We paddled through the now longer straight stretches and around several curves, and after a kilometer there were still no rapids. I told Pablo maybe they had ended. He said *"Esperamos"* (Let's hope so), and we paddled on.

Every so often what looked like a large bluejay flew low and fast a few hundred feet up ahead on the Rio. Pablo said it was a *pescador* or fisherman bird, and that they came out just before it rained, looking for fish. He predicted rain soon, although it was only two-thirty in the afternoon and it didn't usually rain until four or five. We began to get closer looks at the birds, as some flew from behind and right by us, skimming four feet over the water. They were fairly large, with two-foot wing spans, and had mostly blue bodies, with white collars, black heads and robin-red undersides.

Ahead we saw a small ripple across the Rio. It was a tiny cascade. I guessed it was only a foot or so high, so we went on. At its edge, I saw it was over two feet high, but we were already upon it. We slipped over, and went down bow first, drawing some water but not capsizing. I caught a look of fright on Pablo's face as we went over, but when we had made it through safely and he saw me look at him again, he forced a smile. I realized he was still very nervous on the Rio.

Then the rains came. First a light sprinkling for a few minutes, then a tremendous curtain of tropical downpour fell upon us.

I had put on my poncho at the first few drops to protect the movie camera, but Pablo had lost his poncho in the capsize, and was unprotected against the torrential rain. It was lashing him and he was cold. I said we could camp now for the night, or go on until three-thirty, or until the next cascade.

Pablo said it would be better to continue. I felt sorry for him but also confident, as he seemed to be taking heart again. Pablo was strong and brave, but he was afraid of the unknown. He was afraid of the Rio. To him it was *torcido*, cursed, and that meant danger, and danger can mean death.

Since before the dawn of civilization, man has lived in fear of the one great unknown—death. To escape it he has invented gods and religions. The Mayans built a glorious empire which was founded on a fanatical placation of the gods. It was their downfall.

I was going to see a Mayan religious center, to try to capture and re-imagine its glory. A product of modern westernism, I was searching for a mood, but Pablo, a product of ancient mysticisms, was afraid of ghosts. And so bravery, as with all else, is only relative.

My thoughts were snapped back to reality by a sudden, tigerish yell. "*Saraguate!*" Pablo said.

Then I recognized it, as it went on with the second half of its cry, that deep doglike bark. It was up ahead in a tall tree on our right, the same kind of ape we had encountered when we were with Carmen. (Carmen . . . Alcira . . . how far removed those first few days seemed now.)

The rain was so fierce and heavy I couldn't get a good look at the *saraguate* as we paddled by his tree, but he continued to roar and bark as we passed.

Stroke by stroke we went on in the heavy rain. It splashed so loud on the water, we came upon the forty-fifth cascade without realizing it. It was almost too late.

In a frenzy we paddled toward the left bank, which was closer. Grabbing desperately at the bushes along it, we finally came to a stop only five feet from the edge of the cascade. It plunged down ten feet in a solid wall of thundering water.

Pablo jumped out of the boat and quickly tied it to a small tree. I followed and we began to cut our way forward, looking for a good camp site, which we soon found. The rain was still coming down hard.

In the downpour we found a few corozo trees nearby and began cutting long fronds, I doing the best I could with my jackknife. Then, while Pablo put the *champa* together, I searched for firewood and started on the fire. The heavy rain made it difficult, but I finally got it going under the *champa*, and we slung our hammocks around it. I climbed in mine and started to write. Pablo went down to the Rio to try his luck at fishing. He returned half an hour later, saying the bait was not right. The rain had stopped. We lay in our hammocks and talked. He said the fish sometimes ate parrot meat, but preferred chapái or ramón nuts, both now out of season, not ripe and hard to find. I asked him what kind of fish were in the river, and he said only *machaca*. (The Rio got its name from this fish.)

Pablo asked how far we had gone during the day. I said nine kilometers, and added that we had passed fourteen cascades. Then I reminded him that the last five kilometers had only three or four, and it looked as if they would soon end. He said he hoped I was right. So did I. I knew he was near the end of his resistance to the river. When he spoke of it every other phrase seemed to be *Que rio torcido!* Or when I spoke of it he would comment with "*Si, es torcido; muy torcido!*" Trying to break his mood before he talked himself into a depression over it, I changed the subject.

I asked him about his life in Poptún. I already knew he was married and had several children. I asked about his land. He said he had seventy-five *mecates* planted. This was almost 17,-000 square feet, or a plot roughly 250 feet by seventy feet. He said one doesn't buy the land, one just goes out into the jungle, clears it and plants it. It's government land, and as long as you use it it's yours. Except, of course, until the government decides it needs it.

I asked what he had planted. He said it was about equally split up between *maiz, frijoles* and *arroz* (corn, beans and rice). The yield was three *quintals* or 300 pounds of rice per *mecate* and one each of *maiz* and *frijoles* per mecate. The rice he sold for twenty quetzals a quintal, and the *frijoles* for ten. They eat most of the *maiz*, as it is made into tortillas, the staple of their diet, as it is in Mexico. It is thought that *maiz* was an original wild Guatemalan plant.

The Mayan peoples became sedentary, flourished into a great civilization, built their temples, sacrificed victims, and in the end were destroyed as an esthetic culture, because of one thing. *Maiz*. In a word, corn. It had created then ruthlessly abandoned a great civilization, one that had reached the highest degree of culture in the New World. No wonder the Mayans proclaimed it their most important god, calling him *yum kaax*, the corn god.

There have been several theories advanced for the reason of the collapse of the Mayan empire. Taking them into consideration, I now add my own.

Corn was the staple food of Mayan civilization. The Mayans had only a rudimentary knowledge of agriculture, knew nothing of fertilization or turning the soil. When it became unproductive, they simply moved the cornfields to a new spot, abandoning the old wornout field.

As the centuries passed, the cornfields became so far from the ceremonial centers that it was an increasing burden for the farmers to go to these centers on the frequent holy days. Further, they were ignorant and extremely superstitious, putting all their faith in the priests. They looked upon them with awe and fear and virtually considered them gods.

These priests were great mystics and astronomers, and

jealously guarded what they had learned in meditation and observation of the heavens. Of the stars they knew much, but they ignored the science of agriculture. The time came when the cornfields were far from their ceremonial centers and the peasants, who finally realized that the all-knowing priests could not make the old fields productive by imploring the Mayan gods, began to lose faith in their powers.

Human sacrifice became more frequent and brutal. Still the priests could not make the cornfields productive again. Their power was soon lost, and they were no longer held in awe and fear.

Some of the farmers left for new areas, and some practiced civil disobedience. When they were punished for these acts, the peasants began to rebel against the priests and the nobility, many of whom were killed or fled.

The old centers were abandoned, mainly the large ones of the Peten area; no more stelae with their dated inscriptions were carved or erected. Much of the knowledge of the priests was lost forever, and in time it was forgotten as the last priest died in obscurity. The corn withered in the fields, while the priests indulged in fantasies, the nobles lived in luxury and the long-suffering, starving peasants were intimidated, sacrificed and ignored.

The corn god, created by the priests, had abandoned the priests. It was only a mystic's dream. The ground the corn grew in was real. It had been ignored by ignorance, and once again mysticism had destroyed itself by too much self and over indulgence. Reality had proved its point, and only reality remained. Now the temples, those magnificent by-products of mysticism, lay in ruins and the attainments of a great civilization were forever lost. Even the people have been assimilated by other races, although 160 pure Mayans still remain in the jungles of Chiapas, Mexico. Called *lacandones*, after the name of a river that flows through their area, they have reverted to the existence of their pre-Mayan ancestors of several thousand years ago.

But the corn god still reigns in Mexico and Guatamala, and his golden image has entered the houses of the rest of the world. So when you eat corn, again, remember: you are not eating an ordinary food—you are eating a god.

I had been pondering the riddle of the Mayans for some time when Pablo asked what I was thinking about. I said Mayans and corn, and asked him how much he sold a quintal of corn for. He said it only brought two or three quetzals. Too cheap for a god, I thought, and asked him why.

"*Es muy commune,*" (it's very common), he said adding that everyone grows their own and that *arroz* is better.

Another god? I thought in silence. Then I thought again.

The Mayans, like all American Indians, originally came from Asia, where rice is king. Had the lord of rice finally come to proclaim himself once more the god over his long lost children? Or was I getting too mystical? It can happen easily in the jungle: I could see a gigantic battle between the heroic figures of the corn god and a rice god. I had a good idea who would win.

Pablo again noticed my silence. "*Que pasa?*" he asked.

"Nothing," I answered; "I was thinking of gods."

Pablo was quick to say he also believed in *Dios y la Virgen.* I smiled.

Our conversation now turned to the serious matter of logistics. If we didn't find a way to get food from the jungle soon, we would be in bad shape. We only had eight rounds of ammo left, and it was hard to hit anything with my small-caliber pistol. The question of fishing came up. Pablo didn't think the machaca fish would bite on anything but what he had mentioned earlier, and those nuts were out of season. We began discussing what to do after we reached the ruins. Should we continue down that cursed river to the Pasion or return to

Poptún? I was for the former, Pablo for the latter, naturally. The choice was up to me. I said I would make it when the time came, but the Rio Pasion would probably be my choice.

Pablo seemed nervous about that last statement. I said that it would be about six days each way, and probably longer back to Poptún. We could stop each day at one P.M. and fish on the Machaquilá on the way to the Pasion. This was our only chance. Pablo disagreed. Back to Poptún was better, *mucho mejor*, he repeated several times. I said the chance for fish was better than the chance for shooting a bird with only eight rounds on the way back to Poptún. Pablo brought up the nuts-out-of-season again. We were getting nowhere so I changed the subject.

I asked why it was raining so much now that it was almost December. According to the books I had read about the weather in El Peten, the rainy season was at its height in July and August and by November was down to an occasional shower every other day. Pablo smiled. The books lie, he said. I said maybe they were old. He said that might be true, as the weather had been changing the last twenty years. Still, he said, many people lie and exaggerate about the jungle.

But why lie about the weather? I asked. *Gringos*, Pablo said. They lied about everything. Well, I said, they liked to sell more books, but why didn't the scientific men like the archeologists tell the truth? Maybe they did, he said; the weather had been changing.

I asked Pablo if he would give me the weather situation of El Peten for the last twenty years. I told him for once we would get it correct and honest, as I was going to write a book. Pablo got excited and asked if I were really going to write a book about the trip. "*Si*," I said. And I would mention him? he asked. I said he was half the book. Pablo was all smiles. "*Bien*," he said; "*vamonos!*" and began to talk.

Pablo's Spanish was not the best grammatically speaking,

and I was in no position to correct him. I knew that some things didn't sound quite right, but not being sure of the correct phrase I took down his words exactly as he spoke them.

Upon re-reading them for inclusion in the book, I decided it would be better if I left them as they were. After all, Pablo was an old *chiclero*, and is now a farmer, and his speech is authentic, honest and simple. So the following is taken directly from my notebook, with no corrections or changes. The translation however, puts the sentences into more correct grammar.

Pablo Paredes Speaks on Weather and Seasons of El Peten, Guatemala.

Los tiempos del año estanos cambiando. Tres años esta cambiando. Lluvia cinco años atras, mucho invierno de mayo, junio, julio, y septiembre. Terminava in enero. Privavera cominció in enero y bastante. Verano no lluve, es seco, febrero hasta mayo. Eso era cinco años atra. Bueno!

ahora esta cambiando el tiempo, esta asi. Invierno (lluvia) comincia in noviembre y mas o menos termina in diciembre, tal vez. Enero es siempre primavera. Febrero, abril, marzo y mayo, es seco, es verano.

Entonces todos los años differente, differente. Está un clima cheno se comprende. Hay años que invierno entre en un mese, y años en otra mese.

In 1963 invierno entró in mayo. Este ano entro en noviembre, y mayo hasta octubre era seco. Siempre va cambiando. No se sabe quando lluvia y quando es seco. Asi es la selva del Peten. Variable!

(Translation):

The seasons of the year are changing. The last three years have changed. About the rain five years ago. There was much winter (rain) in May, June, July and until September. It used to end in January. Spring would begin in January and enough (That's it). In summer it doesn't rain. It's dry February to May. This was five years back. Good!

Now the seasons have changed. It's like this. Winter (rain) begins in November and more or less ends in December, sometimes. January is always Spring. February, April, March and May are dry, it's summer.

So then, all the years are different. Different. It's a climate that you can't understand. There are years that winter enters in one month, and years in another month.

In 1963, winter entered in May. This year it entered in November, and May to October were dry. It is always changing. One doesn't know when it will rain and when it will be dry. Such is the jungle of El Peten. Unstable!

Pablo said he was finished and I thanked him. He asked if I would really put it in my book. I said yes, and I would make him famous. Pablo smiled broadly. He seemed almost embarrassed, but was very happy about it.

We dried our clothing all night until ten o'clock, and talked about various things. Pablo was in the best humor he'd been in since the first day on the river. In a happy mood and with the first really dry clothes in several days, we went to bed and slept soundly till six the next morning.

I was surprised to see Pablo already up and making the fire. It was the first time he had gotten up before me since we had started on the Rio. It was a good sign.

After a Nu-V bar each, I broke camp and Pablo went into the jungle to look for *cambo*, the heart of a small corozo palm, and good to eat. It is usually located five to ten feet off the ground in the center of the trunk, a soft pulpy mass twelve to eighteen inches long and about an inch and a half wide. When Pablo returned he said he hadn't found any but we were sure to find some sooner or later. I put more air in the boat by mouth and by eight o'clock we left, going along the shore and bypassing the forty-fifth cascade.

We went nearly a kilometer and I was just saying that maybe the cascades had ended when we spotted another ahead. It was an easy one and we carried the boat, loaded and all, over a low twenty-five-foot-wide land bridge and kept going.

Suddenly Pablo shouted, *"Lagarto!"* We had spotted our first alligator, a four-foot baby swimming ten feet ahead. We barely managed to miss it. Down a way I saw two more large ones, the last we would see on the Rio.

Farther downstream, Pablo spotted some *jobo* nuts on a tree. He said the *machaca* sometimes bite on these when they're ripe, and although they weren't now, it would be best to get a few and try them out anyway. They were high up, but with a paddle I finally knocked several down. Most of them fell into the water and sank like lead, but a few fell into the boat. We took one each and carefully put them in our pockets for future use.

We went along for a kilometer and came upon a *tapón* of several trees across the river. They were not a matter of a few years old as the other had been. These trees were large, old and moss-covered, and looked as if they had been rotting there forever. Pablo said they had probably fallen twenty or thirty years before. It was slow going, but we found our way under all of them without too much difficulty.

The Rio was again narrowing down; in some places wasn't more than fifty feet across. The curves were tighter and more frequent, with the straight stretches barely a hundred yards long. We paddled on the currentless waters for two kilometers, and came upon a rapid, at a particularly narrow spot, overhung with trees. It had that dark foreboding look of a tunnel. I looked at Pablo, not wanting to force him into any further predicaments, as the rapid looked very swift. "*Vamonos?*" I asked. Staring ahead at the choppy current, he said, "*Si*," and we entered the fast-moving dark waters.

The rapid was not as bad as it looked, but we couldn't see much in the dim light, and we passed over several submerged sticks and heard them scraping along the bottom of the boat. One stopped us dead and almost came through the floor, but we shifted our weight and passed over it.

Pablo was in fright again. We went along in the rapid and under the low-hanging trees for a few hundred yards. It was beautiful and eerie, my awareness slipping back and forth from one sensation to another.

We reached the end of the tunnel-like rapids and floated into a tremendous complex of *tapóns*. Islands had formed against some as most of the trees were old. The Rio wound in between them like a twisting snake. We had to go over some, hauling the boat across, and under others. It was tedious work and took us the better part of an hour. I counted more than forty trees across or into the Rio at this point.

Continuing downstream for a kilometer, we went into another rapid but it was short and not dangerous. We went ahead for a few hundred meters, and around a bend to the left we suddenly came upon our forty-seventh cascade. It was a land-bridge type with a flow on the left again. We went up against the embankment and while Pablo jumped up onto the bushy land bridge to scout a way through I waited. After awhile I became impatient, and standing up in the boat I grabbed at a bush and started to get up on land.

As I did so the boat sank under my weight and I saw that the left-side air chamber had taken a puncture. I made sure the packs were secure and called for Pablo. We went along the land bridge to the right, dragging the boat along in the water. Then we came to an overflow at the end of the bridge, near the bank. It was a tumbling, cascading slide, twenty feet long.

Below it was a small *laguna* and I spotted a bare bank of earth along its shore. We waded across the overflow and began to cut into the underbrush, trying to go around and reach it through the jungle. The bushes were thick and thorny, and we were attacked by large black ants, which bit us mercilessly. We retreated back to the land bridge, and decided to climb down along it to the *laguna*.

Pablo went down first, and then I pushed the boat to him. He was swimming in the water and pulling the boat as I started down. Halfway down along the rocky slide of water I lost my footing and fell in a pancake dive, striking the water with a stunning splash. Pablo looked back and after I recovered we both laughed.

We swam for a hundred yards and finally reached the spot I had picked out along the bank. It was a steep ten-foot muddy mess but it had a few bushes on it. I chose a spot with a large tree at its top, and after several attempts, Pablo reached it. I untied the packs and handed them to him, then the boat, and then Pablo helped me up.

The jungle above the bank was thin and I had no trouble clearing out a spot to work, while Pablo built the fire. I would have to get the rubber on the boat bone-dry to patch it. I found the hole. It was a two-inch ninety-degree tear at the front of the left tube.

After drying it thoroughly I put a three-inch-square patch over it, waited fifteen minutes and blew it up to half capacity. I waited again and then filled the chamber as full as I could. It made me so dizzy I had to rest a half hour to recover my senses.

The spot we were in was shady and secluded. There was a beautiful view of the laguna and cascade, and the sun had come out brightly. Pablo had gone along the bank to cut a trail, as the next cascade was a hundred meters ahead. When he returned it was noon.

We carried everything along the trail to a point just below the forty-eighth cascade and put the boat in the water. The Rio was narrow but clear for a kilometer, and then we hit a stretch of fast-moving water. There were many sticks in it and it was hard to avoid them. We were both puncture-conscious now. A few hundred yards downstream the current became a rapid and we almost took another puncture. We got hung up on a damn stick and it looked as if we would be sunk for sure, but after a few minutes we managed to get off it with no apparent damage. Our Japanese-made two-man boat seemed almost indestructible; even Pablo was amazed at its strength. With the Rio as bad as it was, a lesser boat would have taken a dozen holes by now.

The rapid ended but the stick hazard continued for several kilometers. The river became dead-calm and it was slow going. It was like an abandoned, unearthly, long snaky-thin lake, instead of a wild Rio.

After awhile the water began to move along at a few kilometers an hour, but the sticks continued, with an occasional tree sticking weirdly out of the water. Pablo was getting increasingly nervous and it showed in his erratic paddling. We had trouble avoiding the sticks, and it led to some short sharp arguments.

The Rio now became forty feet wide, full of sharp curves and sticks, and it began to move faster and faster. The next three kilometers were a tense nightmare. We hit seven rapids, all short but dangerous. The sticks and trees in the water plagued us. We must have hit a dozen head-on, but our boat held up. Pablo began to curse the Rio and he was wild-eyed. He had me more worried than anything else.

To top things off, the rain came down for almost an hour in a heavy deluge, carrying us along even faster in the dangerous waters. We began to crash against the branches and bushes along the banks, and I thought Pablo was going to leap right out of the boat in fright. Twice we almost overturned. Pablo was in a very bad state now. It was only two o'clock and the last kilometer had been fairly clear, but I decided to get off the Rio for the night anyway before he flipped completely.

We pulled over to the left side at a *corozal*. The bank was eight feet high and straight up. We had a hard time making the top, but once there we saw it was worth it. The *corozal* was beautiful and the spot was a good camp site. While Pablo built the *champa* and I slung the hammocks, the rain, which had slacked off before, stopped completely.

Pablo searched the jungles and came back in a half hour. He had found two *cambos*. Then we decided to try out luck at fishing with the two *jobo* nuts we had. Pablo cut one in half and put them on our hooks. We dropped our lines down a foot below the surface and waited. After a few minutes we saw some *machaca* fish, but they didn't seem to care for our bait. We fished for a half hour with no luck. The fish just swam up for a look and darted away again. We were both about to quit when Pablo gave a yank on his line and pulled a beauty up onto the bank. A seventeen-inch *machaca!*

It had half-inch scales on it, was green, speckled with white on top and had a gray belly. The eyes were larger than most fishes'. The thick body curved back into a thin tail, and when Pablo opened the mouth I was almost repulsed. It looked human! The bottom teeth were large molars, while the top row had smaller teeth with a row of still smaller ones behind it. Some of the larger ones on the bottom row were almost as big as a man's molar teeth.

The fish stopped moving after a short time, and in fifteen minutes it was ready to gut and cook. Pablo did this, but before he did I made a quick sketch of it. Then he scaled and gutted it, and made about twenty-five cuts along it on each side. He said it was full of bones and hard to eat if you didn't cut them. When it was done he rubbed salt into the cuts, and roasted it on a spit over the fire. He put the *cambos* at the edge of the hot embers and in twenty minutes they and the fish were ready.

We both ate slowly, savoring every bite. Pablo kept smiling. There were not as many spines as I had imagined, and the flavor was good.

A little after five o'clock, as darkness began to fall, Pablo heard and spotted a large black bird he called *cojolito* up in a tall tree. He pointed it out whispering and I spotted it. It was over seventy-five feet away, sitting nonchalantly on a large limb, and in plain view. I knew it was too small a target with the pistol, but Pablo insisted on trying anyway. I handed him the pistol and with careful aim he fired. The bird flew away.

We now had only seven rounds of ammo left. The fish had whetted Pablo's appetite and strengthened his confidence. He went to the Rio to try his luck again. I sat by the fire and wrote awhile, and in a half hour Pablo returned without any fish. We began to dry our clothes by the fire and talk.

Pablo asked me how far I thought we were now from the ruins. We had gone thirteen kilometers that day and I figured we had fifteen or twenty more to go. Pablo was happy about this but asked if I was sure. I said no, but according to my calculations that must be pretty close to it. I asked him how he would know when we reached the spot opposite the ruins. Pablo said it was impossible to miss. The Rio branched out around an island, and the smaller branch to the left was the one with the ruin. The point where the *arroyo*, as he called the smaller branch, began to cut around the island was called *El Final*. From there it was eight kilometers by land to the ruins. I asked why the spot was called El Final. He said it was the last camp of the geologists of Union Oil.

Pablo again said that from the ruins it would be best to go back to Poptún by land, a trip which he kept insisting would be no more than six days long. I asked him if he had consid-

ered the fact that we had no machetes and no boots to wear.
He said yes. Then I admitted we didn't know how bad the Rio
was below the ruins. Pablo smiled, taking this as a definite yes.
That night we got into our hammocks and went to sleep early.

I woke up several times during the night, restless and
thinking about the ruins. We were only a day or two away, and
after all our tribulations my excitement and expectations were
again beginning to mount. I would sit by the fire stoking it,
smoking and dreaming of the ancient Mayans who had once
called this jungle their home, and whose ritualistic temple
center lay in one of the remotest spots in all the Peten.

Macháca fish (*author's drawing*)

How had they chosen such a place? Was it a lone, secret
center even in their time, and had they fled here for some reason to escape other more populated areas? Was it a center
among other smaller temple cities, or was Machaquilá itself a
known center in its own time and only a satellite to a larger
city such as *Ceibal*, forty miles to the northwest as the *zopilote*
flies? How many other ruins, crumbling and forgotten, not
seen by man in over a thousand years, had we passed on our
journey down the Machaquilá? I was in and out of my hammock all night. Finally at five o'clock I was awake for good.
Pablo was up soon afterward and by six-thirty we were on the
Rio again. We were hoping to make the ruins that day, and
every hour counted.

We paddled hard, and after two kilometers reached a rapid that we slipped swiftly through. Not far beyond it lay a double *tapón* of trees, but they were not difficult. The Rio now began to move slowly but steadily, at one or two miles per hour, and with the paddling we were going at a fair speed of five. The Rio had widened a little, averaging seventy-five feet across. At this pace we went another two kilometers and I told Pablo with luck we'd reach the fork in the river at El Final well before noon. We were both in high spirits.

But the Rio had not done with us yet. After another kilometer, we reached another cascade we had to go around along the shore. Then the old dread began to take hold of us again, as a couple of hundred yards downstream we came upon our fiftieth cascade; then the fifty-first, some 400 yards farther along. It was a very difficult triple-tiered maze of irregular drops, with a total length of about 200 feet. The final drop was so bad we had to unload the boat and portage it a hundred feet around through the jungle. The fifty-second, a half kilometer downriver, was a one-foot step so we chanced it through and made it with no trouble, but not far ahead was a monster!

It was another triple-tiered winding mess of cascades, bushes and islands, with tree trunks strewn through it. We finally managed to get ourselves and the boat through it, but Pablo was completely demoralized. I kept telling him we'd be off the Rio in a few hours and not to worry. He kept saying we'd be dead soon if we didn't get off that cursed river right then. Did it pay to die at the last minute? he asked. I assured him we were not going to die, but he had me worrying too.

We went a kilometer downstream before we reached the fifty-fourth cascade. It was only two feet high so I decided to slip over it. We did and barely made it. The front end of the boat, heavy with our packs, went under, but we only drew ten gallons of water and continued on.

Now the Rio widened to well over a hundred feet and the

curves became fewer. Some of the straight stretches were almost a half kilometer long. The water calmed and we paddled on swiftly, still hoping to reach the ruins before dark. One, two, three kilometers passed with no cascades. I told Pablo the cascades *must* be ended now and urged him to cheer up. He finally smiled and we paddled on with new hope. The thought even came to me that we might continue on to the Pasion after the ruin, but I said nothing about it to Pablo.

After our fourth kilometer ended with no cascades we saw a hill up ahead on the left side of the Rio. Continuing on, we heard and then saw another cascade.

Our fifty-fifth, it was at the base of the hill. It was another very bad triple and I could hardly believe it. Again it was full of bushes growing along the edge of the falls in spots, and interwoven with islands and tree branches. We almost punctured the boat again, getting stuck on a protruding branch. I was sure it would break through the flooring, but after a five-minute struggle we freed ourselves and eventually made it through. . . .

Ahead we heard the roar of another cascade!

Part Four   The Ruin

~~~~~~

1 · END OF THE TRAIL

WHEN WE REACHED the cascade, some 300 meters downstream, Pablo was furious. I didn't blame him. It was the
worst one of the entire trip on the Rio. It was a triple and
there were bushes, islands and torrents of water gushing
around them and breaking through everywhere. The whole
river was strewn with the debris of countless trees that had
fallen into it over the years.

We stopped on an island for a few minutes, looking in awe
and in disgust. Then, making our way to the right shore,
which seemed the best way around, we were attacked by large
black ants. It was impossible to make the shore anyway, as the
bushes were growing right out of the water. Pablo was cursing
and I was disgusted with the Rio myself. We made our way
forward in a maze of bushes, currents and cascades.

My anger was turning to desperation, but Pablo beat me to

it. He began to scream that this was it. We would die right there! We must get off the Rio, now! he shouted. There was no more argument about it.

I'd had it, too, but Pablo's shouts and accusations got to me. He blamed me for everything and began to recite a series of past mishaps, asserting loudly that I had caused them all.

That was too much. We stood there, trapped in the middle of a cascading, churning madness of water, shouting at each other above the clamor of the river, hurling accusations back and forth. After a minute we calmed down, but in the end Pablo said he was sure I wouldn't go back with him to Poptún, as I had promised. I said I hadn't promised anything. He said I had, but asked if I intended to go down the Rio beyond the ruins. He himself was going back to Poptún from the ruins, once and for all. I said I had made no promises or decisions on what we'd do after reaching the ruins, but I stated then and there that we *would* return by land. That stopped the argument cold. Pablo stared at me in disbelief. I reassured him, saying that as soon as we made it through that cascade, we'd get off the Rio.

There's no doubt about it, I thought; *if we don't get off this river now it will kill us.*

Cautiously we struggled on, down through the torrents and bushes. The complex of cascades was only a hundred feet long and thirty feet high but it was extremely difficult and treacherous. It took us an hour to make our way through it with the boat. When we had accomplished the feat we paddled across the Rio and landed on the left bank, about 200 meters below the cascades, and there we abandoned the Rio.

The sun was bright and birds were singing in the jungle around us. I looked back at the cascade, the *fifty-sixth*, and our last! Beautiful from here, I thought, but deadly. I checked my notebook. We had left Poptún ten days before. The date was December first.

Actually we might have gone on, as it was only four or five kilometers by river to El Final, but Pablo had flatly refused to do so during our argument in the cascade. Now he said that if we could find the old trail to the ruins we could make it before dark. After a few minutes he found signs of it. He said it was four kilometers to El Final by this trail, and from there another eight to the ruins.

Pablo built a small *champa* off the trail, while I deflated the boat and put it, the oars and everything we didn't absolutely need at the ruins under it. We had now definitely decided to return to Poptún, so we could pick everything up on our way back from the ruin.

We put on our packs and started out on the overgrown trail toward El Final. It seemed strange to start out on a long march through the jungle. It was the first time we actually had to back-carry the packs. First we'd had the mule, and then the boat, to do the job.

Pablo said the trail had been three meters wide, two years ago, when he had cut it while taking Don Juan to the ruins. Now in places it completely disappeared and Pablo had to cut a way through again. I was amazed that such a wide trail had grown over in such a short period of time. So was Pablo. In some places the cut bushes had grown in faster and thicker than the surrounding jungle and we had to go around them. It was unbelievable.

After an hour my twenty-five-pound pack seemed like fifty. The Rio had not conquered my spirit, but it had weakened me physically more than I had realized. Pablo forged ahead at a fast pace, using his knife to cut through the underbrush as he would have a machete. Once more he was the *hombre de hierro*. The man of iron was back in his element.

Just after noon, Pablo stopped and said we had reached El Final. The only sign of the old camp was a rusting tin can. It was fully overgrown, but Pablo was sure that was it.

Making our way farther along, we came to the Rio again and I spotted the small arroyo coming in around the island. Pablo called it the *arroyo seco* (dry stream) but at this time of the year it was full of water. He said it dried up in March and April. From this spot we had only eight kilometers to go. With mounting excitement, we started out on the last trail to the ruins.

We continued on, following the arroyo southwest. Sometimes we came to within twenty feet of it and through the trees I could see that it was about twenty-five feet wide, moving fast and full of small cascades and rapids. At other times the winding trail took us much farther away and then we moved through a sea of green underbrush.

It soon became apparent that the trail was not only worse than the one to El Final, but almost non-existent. Pablo kept telling me how wide it had been and how impossible it seemed that it had grown over so badly. Sometimes he stopped to look around, and I would ask *"Es el camino?"* (is it the way?). Pablo always answered with *"Si, si, esta bien"* (Yes, yes, it's OK).

We continued on through the thickly grown-in trail, over *tapóns* of trees, through rocky passes at the edge of small *cerros*, and still the trail never cleared. In places it was so thick I began to get the feeling we were lost.

Finally we came to a point that I estimated as eight kilometers from El Final. When I mentioned this to Pablo he said I was about right, and the ruins should be just ahead. A few hundred meters more, he said. When we had gone more than twice that distance, Pablo stopped and looked around, puzzled. I asked if he were sure he could find the ruins.

"Si, creo," he said.

"I think so"? What an answer, I thought. Had I taken a man along through all this who only *thought* he could find the deeply hidden ruins? I said nothing and we continued on, slowly.

After a few more hundred meters, Pablo stopped again, looking around uncertainly. My pack was heavier than ever. The last eight kilometers seemed like twenty. I was beat, but the thought of the ruin's being so near filled me with expectation.

Then Pablo said something that deflated me considerably: maybe we had passed the ruins and should go back a way to look around again. I told him to wait a minute while I rested. I had to think.

I was so exhausted my head was spinning. Obviously Pablo had lost the trail, and was going on instinct alone. I waited a minute and told him that maybe we had miscalculated the distance from El Final. I said we should go ahead another kilometer before we turned back to search for the ruin. (I had a strange, urgent feeling that it was just ahead.)

Pablo said OK and started out again. After a hundred meters, he suddenly turned to the right, hurriedly broke through the jungle and disappeared among the leaves. I followed him as fast as I could. After a hundred feet the jungle began to thin and I found Pablo standing in a sort of clearing.

He smiled. "*Estamos in las ruinas!*" (We are in the ruins!) he said.

I broke out into a grin but I was still skeptical. "Where are they?" I asked.

"They start a hundred meters over there," he said, pointing to the left; then, walking to the right, he said Don Juan's old camp had been there.

The remains of a rotting *champa* proved his point. He said he'd show me the *arroyo seco*, and we found it thirty feet farther on. A fifteen-foot arroyo was behind another decaying *champa*. Along it was an old Mayan wall.

A sudden thrill of adventure came over me. It was four
o'clock. I told Pablo to see if he could repair the better
champa a little and make camp. I wanted to go to the ruins to
see them before it got dark. He said there was time in the
morning and we could go together. I said I knew that, but I
was going over for a quick look. I wanted to stand in them
alone for awhile. Pablo pointed out the direction again and
told me approximately where I would find the stelae and the
sacrificial table. I started out.

I cannot describe my excitement. Visions came to me as I
crashed on through the jungle. My heart began to pound.
Huge trees formed a solid canopy high overhead. It was dark
and mysterious and there were no sounds except those of my
feet crunching along.

Suddenly the underbrush ended and I stepped forward
into an even darker area. Before me lay a tumbled mound of
cut stone. It was covered with leaves, and small trees grew everywhere on it. For a moment I stood there in a daze. Then,
tense and expectant, my heart seeming to beat even harder, I
started up it.

The loose stones shifted, and some cut my feet through
the *pita* sandals, but I went on, occasionally checking some
stones to see if they were carved. I found none. I finally made
the top, and with all my senses tuned to a high pitch, I looked
around through the jungle.

From my vantage point I could see above the lower jungle
underbrush. Ahead of me stood another ruin mound. Then I
spotted two more to the right and, turning, another to the left.
They all stood between thirty and fifty feet high and were
formed like the one I stood on, which was only forty feet high.
The base of my temple mound was about ninety feet long and
the top I now stood on was about fifty feet long. It was not
flat, but more like a rounded ten-foot ridge. Obviously the
temples that had been on top had crumbled and the form was

now more that of an irregularly shaped hill than of a temple pyramid.

I looked down the other side to see if I could see any stelae, for Pablo had said that there were some. Then I remembered he had said the second temple. I made my way to the bottom and, searching the jungle underbrush, found nothing. I started up the second temple mound. It was shaped like the first. From its top I spotted another pyramid to the left. I had now spotted six in all.

I went down the other side of the pyramid and began to search for the stelae Pablo had mentioned. They were, he had said, lying flat on the ground. The underbrush was thick and I couldn't find them. I decided to get back to Pablo as it was already growing dark.

I started up the second pyramid mound again. Near the top I spotted a stone different from all the rest. I examined it. It was twenty inches long, had four flat sides, and while one end was five inches square, the other end tapered to four inches. It was pitted and there were no traces of inscriptions that might have been carved on it but I picked it up and took it with me. I knew it was rare, as I had never seen or read anything about a stone with such a shape. It was limestone and weighed about fifteen pounds.

I decided to take a look at the last temple mound I had seen to the left. Now it was to my right. I was keeping every direction in mind, so as not to lose my way. It is very easy to get lost in the jungle, and I didn't even have Pablo's compass. The thickness of the trees and underbrush retards sound, and a loud yell cannot be easily heard for more than a few hundred yards.

The mound I was heading for lay only a couple of hundred feet away. Its appearance was the same as the others. I scouted it and, climbing down the far side, decided it was best to start back to Pablo and the camp.

I walked ahead in what I thought was his direction, but after 200 meters or so I didn't recognize where I was. I decided I had veered off to the right too much and started off again, heading farther left. It was getting darker and a grayness began to descend through the trees around me. I reached a temple mound unexpectedly and it surprised me. I didn't know which one it was. Climbing it, I could only spot one other mound through the jungle tangle. I had gone completely off course. Fear came over me. It was getting darker and darker.

Putting down my stone, I cupped my hands and gave a loud yell, then listened. Nothing. I yelled again, the sound not seeming to carry through the trees at all. No answer. I had no idea in which direction Pablo was or how far away he might be. In my excitement among the ruins I had gotten all turned around. I was lost! I had a brief moment of panic, and then in desperation yelled again, very loud. No answer. I tried all directions, giving several more yells. My fear was growing when suddenly I heard something like a low, distant moan. I yelled loudly in its direction. Again I heard a distant sound. I recognized it as a human call and started toward it in great relief.

After a hundred meters I called out Pablo's name. "Ho! Aqui!" Pablo's call came back. It took me another hundred yards to reach him. We both grinned as I approached. He asked if I had gotten lost. I said yes. He reminded me he had told me to wait until morning. The jungle, he said, had killed many men who underestimated it. I said I would remember that. Then I heard some voices above us in the trees.

2 · MONKEYS AND MAYAN GHOSTS

PABLO AND I walked toward the arroyo and suddenly he stopped, motioning for me to be quiet. "*Monos,*" he said, pointing up into the treetops.

At first I saw nothing; then I saw one, then another and another, as they began to leap from branch to branch, chattering again. There were about eight or nine black and white monkeys up there. I asked Pablo what they were called, and he said *micos* and told me to try to shoot one as they were good eating. I didn't mind shooting at birds for food, but I wasn't too keen on killing a monkey.

"*Tira,*" Pablo said, "*Tira!*" (Shoot!). I said they were too far up. Pablo wanted me to try anyway. He said we needed food badly. He was right. Even if we cut down to half rations, we only had a four- or five-day supply left, and Pablo said it was a six-day forced march back to Poptún. I took out my pistol and taking careful aim, fired at one of the monkeys a hundred feet above us in the branches.

There was a series of high-pitched shrieks while the *micos* scurried back and forth among the branches. I fired again. Again I missed, and again they shrieked and leaped about. I said they were too far away and the pistol was no good. Pablo asked permission to use it and I handed it to him. He fired once and missed. By now there were only four or five monkeys left; the others had leaped away through the treetops. I told Pablo not to waste another shot, but he fired anyway. Again he missed. He shook his head and handed the pistol back to me, saying they were too far away. We only had three rounds left now. Pablo said that was bad, but assured me we were bound to shoot a bird on the way back to Poptún. I hoped he was right.

It was now after five o'clock and almost dark. We returned to the *champa* and I opened our last can of corned beef, partly in celebration of our arrival at the ruin and partly to try to make Pablo feel better. He kept saying what a good meal we had missed with the monkeys. We had been living on almost nothing but Nu-V bars for days. The corned beef tasted good.

After eating, I went to the arroyo and washed off the stone I had found at the ruins. Pablo asked what I was going to do with it. I said I was taking it back. Too heavy, he said. Maybe so, I said, but I wanted something, and if I didn't find anything better, I was taking it. Pablo just shook his head. *Mucho pesado*, he said. Too heavy.

Then he asked me if I had found the stelae and the altar. I said I had found nothing, except that I had seen six temple mounds in the area. I asked how many there were. Pablo said he wasn't sure, but that seemed about right. He was quick to add that he was sure he could find the one with the six stelae and the altar in front of it. Pablo said we should go to the ruins very early the next morning, as it would be best to leave for Poptún no later than ten o'clock. I wanted to stay another day, but I didn't insist. Our food supply was already too low for comfort.

If the old trail wasn't better than it had been on the way to the ruins, we were in for a bad trip. At the time I had no idea what an underestimation Pablo had made on the return trip, but even so I had to agree. Still I kept hoping to find a way to stay another day.

I pulled my pack over by the fire and checked our remaining food stores. We had left fifteen Nu-V bars and a can of pemmican. A full daily ration for one man was four Nu-V bars. These four bars, each weighing an ounce and a half, would supply all the vitamins, one-third of the proteins and one third of the calories a man needs daily.

Pablo had been eating four or five daily on the Rio, as he had done most of the work, but I had been limiting myself to two. For a week's time I figured that we could get by with only two each with no ill effects, except a little hunger. Also we could expect to find at least a dozen *cambo* and possibly that many *pacaia* shoots. This was a plant he said grew scattered through the jungle. It was a long flower bud, rich in nutrients. The *cambo* had almost no food value, he said, but filled the stomach and stopped hunger cramps. We might even hit a bird with the three rounds we had left but I couldn't count on it.

I figured our daily food diet for seven days, adding one for good measure to Pablo's six-day estimate. It was simple but bleak! One Nu-V bar each daily, hopefully supplemented by an occasional *pacaia* or *cambo*. The small can of pemmican had 700 calories, but as food wasn't as good as two Nu-V bars.

There was no possible way to stay an extra day at the ruins. We were four or five days behind our schedule already, and had lost almost half of our food supply in the capsize.

Our situation was desperate, and to stay another day would be suicide. As determined as I was, and even reckless in some situations, I had no choice but to leave as early as possible the following morning, after a brief look at the ruins. The thought lay heavy on me but there was no alternative.

I sat staring at the fire. Finally Pablo asked me if we were leaving early the next morning. He said if we left at ten o'clock we could reach the *champa* where we had left the boat by three in the afternoon, and do some fishing. We must find more food, he said.

"*Va bien,*" I said sadly; "We leave at ten in the morning." Pablo said he knew how I felt, but that was how it was.

He had been cutting up his leather *chalveque* bag to make

sandals for me and himself. This would save time in the morning. He worked slowly and carefully. As he did, he began asking me questions about the ruins and the ancient Mayans. It was the first time he had showed any real interest in either, and in the mysterious atmosphere of the ruin, I found it easy and fascinating to tell him what I knew on the subject.

He asked if I knew how old it was. I said it was at least a thousand years old, but that most likely some of the structures were twelve hundred or more years old.*

I said that the six temple pyramids indicated that Machaquilá was a large city. No doubt there were several more structures like them around in the jungle. The size of the now tumbled pyramids showed that it was either the main ceremonial center or one of a complex of temple groups.

How many people had lived there? Pablo asked. I told him that these temple sites were only used by the priests and nobles, but that between 5000 and 10,000 people must have lived around it in the jungle to support such a group of temples. If what I had seen today was only one of a group of temple areas, it was possible that as many as 50,000 people had supported the center and worshiped there.

Pablo asked me what I knew about the people themselves. I said then as now, *maiz* was the biggest part of the ancient Mayan diet. They also ate beans, squash, pumpkins and the yellow yam (sweet potato). For fruit they had papayas and avacados. Pablo asked about bananas. I told him the Mayans had no bananas, as the Spaniards had brought them. And rice? Pablo asked. No rice, but they ate a variety of birds for meat and also tapir and danta. And coffee? I said there was no coffee in Central America at that time. In fact, there was none in the

* I later found out that two of the Machaquilá stelae had been read and dated as A.D. 741 and A.D. 815 (Goodman-Thompson Correlation), by Ian Graham, the man Pablo called Don Juan.

New World. But they did have cacao beans to make chocolate with.

I said that actually even the cacao was rare and that it was sometimes used as money. A pumpkin was worth four cacao beans, and that was what it took to make a cup of chocolate (cocoa). A rabbit or pheasant was worth ten or fifteen beans, and even a slave could be bought for a hundred. I said that I had also read that the price of a woman in a bordello was five to ten beans, depending. Better to buy her as a slave for a hundred, he said. Smiling I admitted he had a point there.

As for clothing, the Mayans had cotton, in fact two kinds, and most of their clothes were made of cotton. They also raised sisal for rope and sandals. On ceremonial days the priests wore clothes woven with feathers and also animal skins. Mainly those of *El tigre grande* (the jaguar), I said, (there are three large Central American jungle cats—jaguar, puma and ocelot, all called *tigre* by the people; the jaguar is the largest).

Pablo's curiosity, now that he saw I knew something about the ancient Mayan, was insatiable. He continued to ask me question after question. How many Mayans were there? he asked. Some authorities say two million, some place the figure over ten million, I said; my estimate was that they were between three and five million Mayans at the height of the empire. As for cities, I said, there are about 250 known sites, but it is estimated that another one hundred or more the size of Machaquilá remain undiscovered.

Pablo found that hard to believe. I said it was true. As large as Machaquilá? he asked. I said Machaquilá was one of the smaller sites and that at least a hundred of the known ruins were larger. I asked if he had heard of Chichen-Itza. No, he said. Copan? No. Tikal? Yes, Pablo had heard of Tikal: "*Es grande, no?*" I told Pablo that the temple complex of

Tikal spread out for eight kilometers in every direction. I went on to say that there was a temple there over seventy meters high. Pablo thought that was impossible.

In Nueva York Estados Unidos, where I come from, I said, there was a building almost *five hundred* meters high. Pablo almost laughed out loud. He said that was surely impossible. I said I wished I had a picture of it. Pablo said he would like to see it, and added he thought I liked to tell stories.

I didn't want to destroy Pablo's confidence in what I had told him about the Mayans, so I said that I would swear on anything he wanted me to that there was a building that tall in New York. He pulled a chain out of his pocket with a cross on it. I held it and swore. For a second Pablo looked shocked, then he said he believed me and smiled. I smiled and told him it was true. I said it was called the Empire State Building and was the highest in the world. He said he had no doubt of that.

Pablo had finished my sandals sometime before, so I tried them on, tying them with rope. They fit fine. It was late, he said, so he would make his in the morning; better to go to sleep now so we could get up early. I agreed and after a cigarette we got into our hammocks.

Pablo fell right off to sleep, but I couldn't. I lay there thinking, knowing that the ruins of an ancient city lay around us in the darkness. I had the disquieting feeling that out there in the jungle shadowy figures of old Mayan priests stood, on the tops of their temples, watching. Every sound out of the darkness seemed magnified. Once I was sure I heard someone walking through the jungle, very close. Then I heard a flurry of steps through the leaves. I rose up in my hammock, wide-eyed. After a minute I heard nothing more and relaxed. I told myself it was only dew, trickling off some leaves. I told myself there were no such things as ghosts, and I knew it. Finally I dozed off.

Suddenly I woke up with a start. I was in a cold sweat. My

heart was pounding. I had heard a voice out there. Then I heard it again and my hair stood up on my scalp. I listened intently. The jungle seemed completely silent, but then I heard it again. This time I recognized it. Those damned monkeys, I thought. It was the *micos* we had seen near the arroyo, just before darkness came. The ones we had shot at, I thought. Were they angry, possibly wounded, did they know we were still around? Would they attack? They were fairly large-sized, I knew. I decided I was being foolish.

They began to chatter more frequently and by now I was wide awake. I checked the time. It was three in the morning. It seemed as if I had only dozed off for a few moments, and six hours had passed. I decided to get up, light the fire, and wait for daybreak at five. Pablo was sound asleep.

As I built the fire and the monkeys continued to chatter high up in the trees, I occasionally looked out into the black jungle. I had the feeling that someone or something out there was still watching me. Those Mayan ghosts again, I thought. My imagination was ready for anything. Those monkeys, high above the ruins in the treetops, might be the Mayan priests, transfigured and watching over their city. But I decided it would not have been their choice. The priests would have chosen the jaguar to house their spirits in. It was one of their gods and, like them, fierce and uncompromising. King of the Peten jungle.

It was going over to check the packs with my flashlight when something on the ground stopped me dead. I whirled around, shining the light around me through the thick leaves. Nothing. I crouched down to check what I had seen again. There was no doubt. In the wet ground beyond the fire there were two *tigre* tracks! They were as large as my fist. "*Jaguar!*" I said, almost out loud. I looked all around the camp on the ground. The great cat had paid us a visit during the night. Luckily it had been just a social call. He had been near the fire, around both Pablo's and my hammock, and it appeared he had gone over to my pack. Just checking us out, apparently.

As I studied his movements by the tracks left, I kept a keen eye out around me in the jungle. I found about a dozen tracks, and then I went back and sat by the fire, thinking about the ruins. Every now and then I would look back over my shoulder as the thought came to me that a *tigre* or an old Mayan ghost was behind me. I kept telling myself to forget it, but I was glad when dawn finally began to lighten things up.

But it was more frightening than ever. The blackness turned into a deep blue-gray, and strange forms began to appear among the leaves and branches. I imagined figures and large animal faces among them. They seemed to twist strangely and move around me, and once I saw a pair of eyes gleam out from the darkness, reappear and then disappear. At this point I had reached for my pistol. *Tigre* or ghost, I was taking no chances.

For a half hour I sat nervously by the fire looking and listening, until finally at five-thirty things began to take their normal shapes again in the daylight. Now that the experience was over I told myself how childish I had been. I lit a cigarette and relaxed. The ghosts had gone with the dawn and, as the chattering up in the trees had stopped so had the monkeys.

3 · MACHAQUILÁ

PABLO WAS UP at six and soon was busy at work making his sandals. It was a beautiful morning, cool and bright, with a few sunbeams coming down here and there through the high canopy of trees. Birds were calling through the jungle, and although it hadn't rained during the night the leaves were shiny with dew.

I remembered the *tigre* tracks and showed them to Pablo. He was impressed but didn't seem disturbed: sometimes they're dangerous and sometimes they're not, he said. He was surprised, though, that the jaguar had come so close, remarking that usually they keep their distance but if they do come that close they may attack. He went back to making his sandals; it would take an hour or so.

I went over to the arroyo, filled the canteen and began to examine the ancient Mayan wall built along it. I was looking for carved stones. I found none. Then I sat down on it, watching the slowly moving water go by and thinking of how the ruins would look again, with Pablo to point out the stelae and temple mounds to me. By eight we were ready to go.

Pablo led the way toward the mound where he said the stelae lay, and after a scant hundred feet or so began to bear right. The way was thick with bushes and small saplings. This had all been cleared when he had been there with Don Juan and was surprised how quickly it had grown over. We continued through the thick foliage. Pablo said the first temple pyramid was on our left now but I couldn't see it through the trees.

Soon we began to circle left and he said we would reach the stelae in a few minutes. The old excitement of discovery was mounting quickly. We could now see the top of the tree-shrouded pyramid to the left, as we circled it. A minute later Pablo stopped and began to hack away at the underbrush. He had found the first stele.

It was lying face down, barely visible under a blanket of plants. I stepped on it and walked along it. It was over ten feet long and this side didn't have the trace of any carvings on it. Pablo began to search for the other four in the area. As he did

I looked around, and my thoughts jumped back and forth between past and present.

This was what I had driven 5000 miles for, and unexplored ruin, lost for a millenium. This was the place I had risked my life to see, across and down 153 kilometers of unexplored jungle and river. This was Machaquilá!

It filled a huge empty spot on my map of Mayan ruins and was the one that I knew must lie in that void on the map. Void not only of ruins, but of towns as well. Poptún was the closest town, and it had taken us eleven days of unrelenting struggle to reach Machaquilá.

As for other ruins, the nearest one was *Ceibál*, to the northwest and up on the Pasión, and a week's journey away by river. *Pusilá* lay to the southeast, over forty airline miles across unknown jungles, where not even the rivers were marked. The only other route was back to Poptún and then a three-day march. To the south was the ruin of Concuén, thirty air miles away near the headwaters of the Rio Pasión. These were Machaquilá's closest neighbors.

Even from its position on a map, one is amazed at the ruin's remoteness, and having made my way there, I now could imagine no spot on earth being in a location more hostile or more hidden from civilization.

Who were these priests who founded such a city? I wondered. Even in the ancient Mayan world, this would have been an out-of-the-way spot. Again I wondered if it had been known, and if it had intercourse with other Mayan temple centers; or had Machaquilá always been a hidden city? No one may ever know for sure.

I tried to imagine the city as it had been over a thousand years ago, with priests and nobles walking around the gleaming white limestone pryamids and temples, framed against their backdrop of green jungle.

For miles throughout the jungle the farmers lived, tending

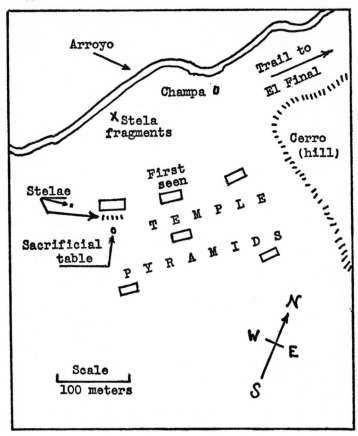

Map of ruins of Machaquilá

their *milpas*, coming here to worship and finally dying, never having left the Machaquilá jungle area. I contemplated that for a minute . . . people living and dying in this remote area of the world and never knowing anything else but jungle, and more jungle. Had it been a paradise or a place of terror? I wondered if it hadn't been a little of both, as I had found it to be.

A dozen times a year or more, thousands of Mayans had gathered in the plazas to listen to the priests and occasionally witness a sacrificial ceremony. I could almost see them milling about, hear their chorused prayers on the command of the priest, that feather-and-jade-bedecked demi-god, high up on the pyramids at the temple doors. . . .

Now it was all crumbling tree-engulfed ruins, barely known to a handful of archeologists, with myself only the second visitor in over a thousand years! As I stood there, deep in the shadow of the main temple, I was amazed at this last thought.

Suddenly I came back to reality and I noticed that the place didn't look familiar. I had not been at this temple mound the day before, when we first arrived at the ruins. Getting my bearings, I decided that this was one of the mounds to the right of the first one I had climbed. Pablo confirmed this when I asked about it, but said that this was the only temple mound with stelae in front of it.

One by one he found the other four stelae, all in a row but the plants and trees had grown in so thick it took him fifteen minutes. And this in a space of only a hundred feet!

They all lay face down along the base of the temple mound. Pablo said that was how Don Juan found them. He raised them with hydraulic jacks to make latex molds of them and then laid them back, face-down again. I knew he had done this to keep them from getting weatherworn and pockmarked, from the rain dripping down from the trees.

The longest of the stelae was easily twelve feet in length, and the two shortest seven or eight. As they were impossible to turn over and photograph, I asked Pablo where the sacrificial table was.

La mesa, (the table) as he called it, was another fifty feet beyond the stelae. At first I saw only a tangle of limbs, which Pablo said he had placed there to protect the top, but as we cleared them the table emerged, covered with dead leaves. Carefully and with excitement we cleared it, until finally its white, carved top was clean. It was beautiful!

I measured it at eighty-six by fifty-four inches. The raised seal in the center held the kneeling figure of a priest surrounded by glyph carvings. This center took up most of the area and was eleven inches thick, the protruding flanges being two inches thinner. This sacrificial altar was raised off the ground on four round columns, twelve inches in diameter and varying from fourteen to twenty inches out of the ground. I took out my movie camera, and as the table was almost three feet off the ground and there was no tree nearby to gain a better view, I photographed the top as best I could from ground level. Then I panned shots of the temple mound and general area and also of two of the stelae. I returned to the sacrificial altar and, stepping upon it, made a quick sketch of it in my notebook. I wanted to do it more justice, but it was almost nine-thirty and if we were to keep our urgent schedule, we had to leave by ten o'clock. After a long, studied look at the table, I helped Pablo recover it as we had found it. I turned and gave one last look around and we headed back for our camp.

On the way back, Pablo made a short detour off our trail, and fifty feet back in the jungle showed me the only standing stele at the ruin. Carved with a priest figure, it was well worn, tilted forward at an angle, only five feet high. Even so I was particularly happy to see the face of at least one of the Machaquilá stelae. After I photographed Pablo next to it, we continued on to camp.

There I asked Pablo if he knew of any small carved stones anywhere that I could take back as mementos. He said maybe he could find some he remembered along the arroyo. We followed it for almost 200 meters until finally we came to a small clearing. There Pablo searched and found some pieces of a broken stele on the ground. There were eight pieces in all, some weighing more than twenty-five pounds each, and all carved with glyphs.

I picked out three of the smallest, weighing four, two and two pounds respectively, wanting to save weight, but it happened they were also the best carved. Returning to camp, I washed them in the arroyo, wrapped them carefully in a towel and placed them in my frame pack. I put the fifteen-pound stone I had found at the ruins the day before at the base of a large tree, between two of its spreading roots. It was really too heavy to take, and now I had better and lighter stones, but I left it reluctantly. It was rare and had been my own find.

I was taking a last shot of the sight with my movie camera, when I heard a *snap* inside the mechanism. The main spring had finally broken, and my last camera was now useless. There would be no more picture-taking.

Shortly after ten o'clock we were ready to leave. As we shouldered our packs I took one last, regretful look around. Then I began to follow Pablo out of the ruins.

My mission had been accomplished. I had seen a Mayan ruin, deep in the jungle, but had paid a terrible price in hardships. And the worst was still ahead.

Part Five   # The Return

~~~~~~

1 · THE IMPOSSIBLE TRAIL

As WE MADE our way back along the trail we had cut coming into the ruins, my heart was heavy. I hated to leave the ruins after such a brief stay, yet without food there was no choice. Ahead lay an uncertain trail through a hundred miles of unexplored jungles.

On such a trip many dangers threatened, some known, some unknown. But the thing that worried me most was wondering whether the trail was open up ahead. We were heading into a possible death trap. But the choice was not ours; the only possible way out was to go at a forced-march pace, sunup to sundown.

Time was still the key factor, balanced against food and energy, with endurance and courage our only variables. I knew I would not give up, and I had great faith in Pablo, the man of iron. But with no machetes to cut a way through the tangled vegetation, with only makeshift sandals on our feet, with inadequate food supplies and unexplored territory ahead, we were attempting an impossible feat, I feared.

Pablo, having more knowledge about what we were attempting than I, forged ahead at a terrific pace and at times I broke into a short trot to keep up with him. I had already decided never to ask him to slow down and never to stop for a rest until he did first. It was his domain, his jungle, but I knew I would have to match his endurance, with my own or I would only further endanger our already almost hopeless situation.

We continued at a relentless pace for two hours, when suddenly Pablo came to a stop ahead of me. I went up to him and asked him what was wrong. Were we resting? Whispering, he said he had seen a *faisano* up ahead through the trees. He asked for the pistol and I handed it to him. He disappeared through the underbrush, and not wanting to take off my pack, I got to my knees and let its weight just rest on my shoulders.

Pablo returned in five minutes; I had heard no shot. He hadn't known how to cock the pistol, and when he finally figured it out the bird had flown away. Then I remembered not having cocked it, when I loaded in the first three rounds at the ruins. We had missed a sorely needed supply of food. I remembered that most misfortunes occur because of bad planning and oversights, and cursed my last one. Pablo said it was *mala suerte* (bad luck), and hoped we would catch a fish when we reached the Rio.

We started off again at a quick pace. Without a break we continued on as before, until at three-thirty we reached the point on the Rio where we had left the boat. The Rio Machaquilá looked like an old friend to me, but Pablo was still cursing it and blaming it for our present situation. I suppose he had a point, but I blamed no one but myself.

Relaxing for awhile after the long march, I had a Nu-V bar and Pablo ate two. That left us with only twelve. Then we both began to fish for the elusive *machacas* in the Rio, using raw chapai nuts as bait.

The spot we chose had large trees along it, making a secluded shady area over the water. A few hundred yards above us on the Rio the last cascade we had passed added a lulling hum to the beauty of the scene.

We patiently fished until almost dark but had no luck. A few fish had come to look at our bait, but didn't even bother to bite. We had to stop and hurriedly build a *champa* and sling our hammocks for the night. Then Pablo built a fire and, smiling, dug into his pack and produced a handful of *pacaia* shoots he had found at the ruins just before we left. I was delighted as I had thought we would go to bed without supper.

Pablo placed a half dozen of the ten-inch flower shoots along the edge of the fire, and in ten minutes they were done. They had an unpleasant bitter taste, but I ate three or four, knowing I would have to get used to anything and everything edible that we could find on the way back.

Sitting by the fire, I asked Pablo his estimate of the return trip's time to Poptún. He said if the trail was not overgrown too badly, about five or six days. And what if it was overgrown? If it were badly overgrown, he said, it would be impossible without a machete.

For a minute I was stunned. I asked what he meant by impossible. We could still keep going by compass, couldn't we? With no machetes, through virgin jungle? was his response. We must just keep going, I said firmly, no matter what.

"Si," Pablo said, "but . . ." He didn't have to finish the sentence.

The rest of the evening we fell silent. Think yourself into the position of a fifty-fifty chance for life and death and you can imagine the thoughts that were running through our minds.

Shortly before eight, Pablo got into his hammock. I stayed up another half hour, looking at the fire, alone with my thoughts. Then I turned in. A few hours later I woke up, cold and shivering. I got the fire blazing again and dried my socks. I wasn't sleepy and stayed up until almost two in the morning, thinking about the predicament we were in, before I finally went to sleep again.

We both slept until after daybreak and got up at six A.M. The first thing I did was to unsling my hammock. Then I repacked my frame pack, checking the contents as I did. I thought I had an extra pack of cigarettes somewhere inside, but I couldn't find it. I checked the open pack in my shirt pocket. There were only seven cigarettes left. Pablo had a corncob pipe that I had given him when we left Poptún, and a handful of tobacco, but he had been smoking my cigarettes since we entered the jungle. Now suddenly, they were almost gone. Another oversight, and another blow to my morale.

I went over to the *champita* under which we had laid the rubber boat and oars. Together they weighed twenty pounds. With the carved stones I had gotten at the ruin, my pack now weighed a good thirty pounds, and Pablo's was at least twenty. I told Pablo that if he wanted the boat and the oars, he could take them as *regalos* (gifts) but that I didn't intend to carry them and I wouldn't ask him to carry them. At this point every pound was an added burden and we both knew it. Pablo smiled and said he was sorry he couldn't accept my *regalo*. I told him it was OK and I would give him most of my equipment anyway when we reached Poptún.

When we reached Poptún, he said, and we both fell silent at the thought of the trail that lay ahead. If there *was* a trail ahead. . . .

I looked at the old rubber boat that had served us so well

on that *rio torcido,* and with us had conquered it. "How long
will it last?" I asked Pablo. He said it would rot in a year. A
sad end for a tough companion, I thought, and we returned to
camp.

The sandals Pablo had made for us had slipped loose on
the trail the day before, and half the time I had been walking
on my heels. Still, they were better than nothing. I re-tied
mine tightly on and at eight o'clock we started out again on
the trail.

My frame pack and my sandals began to hurt after a short
time but I did not mention it to Pablo. We continued on
along the trail, which was overgrown but still visible. After
what seemed like hours of pain, I had to stop shortly after nine
o'clock to readjust my pack and sandals. We split a cigarette
and started out again.

We were moving parallel to the river, usually only twenty
feet away, and occasionally I caught a glimpse of it through
the trees. Then we hit a swamp. We couldn't chance going
around it as the old trail lay across it now, so slipping and
sliding through mud and water which sometimes reached our
waists we started through.

In the swamp the light was dim, the odor of rotting vegetation foul. We skirted around channels of water through
ankle-deep muddy shoals, only to get torn by spines and tangled in vines. Without machetes we were unable to fight back.
At times, yielding to these relentless tortures, we plunged
chest-deep into the channels of unknown waters and waded
ahead in desperation.

Pablo said if I saw a snake to ignore it. Keeping my eyes
dead ahead, I spotted only two but expected at every step to
feel one of them strike at my unprotected feet. What other
monsters lay hidden in the muddy waters of the swamp I
dared not think. I simply followed Pablo, splash after uncertain splash.

After an uneasy half hour, we gained higher, drier ground. I was weak with fatigue but relieved. Without a break Pablo crashed on through the jungle. He was as tall as I, five-foot seven, but at a 135 I must have outweighed his tough, wiry frame by ten. This man of iron was amazing.

Soon the trail began to bear right and inland, away from the Rio. It was the last we would see of it. After less than a kilometer the trail disappeared completely. Pablo told me to wait while he made a circle to try to cross and locate it and disappeared through the thick leaves. I was alone.

I sat down and without unslinging my pack, I leaned back and rested against it. Then I took out my pad and started to write some notes. A two-inch black beetle fell on it as I was writing and I brushed it away. When Pablo had been gone fifteen minutes I began to get nervous. When a half hour had passed and still no Pablo, fear and mistrust hit me. Had he left me behind as dead weight? But he has no food, I thought. Then it came to me with unnerving impact: I had given Pablo eight of the eleven Nu-V bars we had left just before we broke camp that morning. He was eating more than I was, and I figured it would make him feel better if I left him on his honor and didn't ration them out to him.

For awhile I sat there stunned. I tried to put the thoughts out of my mind by feeling my toes and heels, telling myself how much they hurt. The cord between my toes had cut an aching groove, and my heels were full of spines, but I didn't seem to feel anything. I tried to spot a bird that was singing nearby but couldn't. I looked at my watch again. Pablo had been gone for over an hour.

I began to figure what my next move would be, now that I had been left alone to die in the jungle, when I heard a faint call. It sounded human! I shouted as loud as I could. I waited. One, two, three, four minutes passed. Then I heard another call. This time I knew it was human. I called back loudly and sat down, exhausted by tension. After another five minutes, I again heard a call and answered.

A few minutes later I heard something coming through the jungle. I called but no one answered. I reached into my shirt for my pitsol. Then Pablo came into view through the trees. He was smiling and I smiled back. I asked him what had taken him so long. He said it had been difficult, but he finally found the trail. He had a suspiciously embarrassed look about him and I didn't question him further. Later events were to prove that my suspicions and fears had not been unfounded. Even then I was plagued by the thought that Pablo had abandoned me and then changed his mind: An added burden to add to my worries, but there it was and I had to live with it.

We continued for several hundred yards to the point where he had found the trail. We followed it for several more hundred yards, when it ended abruptly. Pablo was at a complete loss. He checked the compass and said he didn't think it was the right trail. Maybe an old *chiclero* trail, he said.

Again he left me to search for signs of what he might recognize as the old trail, but this time he returned in ten minutes looking dejected. This was definitely not the trail he knew that led back to Poptún, he said. The only thing to do was to recross the swamp and try to locate the trail again beyond it.

By compass we headed directly for the swamp, and when we reached it sometime later I shuddered. We were being forced to repeat a nightmare, but this time we were so worried about finding the trail that the swamp didn't seem quite as bad.

By now my pack and sandals were killing me, but I said nothing. Pablo had enough on his mind. He had set a new course back through the swamp and it was worse than before.

We were enshrouded and entangled by all sizes of vines and constantly torn by spines. When finally we had crossed the swamp, Pablo again went off to search for the trail.

Every time he left now, I worried whether he would return or not. I could not tell him of my mistrust: that would only worsen an already bad situation, and he might really get disgusted and leave me.

I sat down, began to write and had one of the five cigarettes we had left. Awhile later Pablo returned, but he wasn't smiling this time. He said he had found the trail all right, but it was very badly *montado* (overgrown).

In low spirits we started out on it and after half an hour reached a somewhat swampy *corozal*. We rested for a few minutes, split a Nu-V bar, and had a smoke on Pablo's pipe. As we smoked, he told me the trail led to a place called *Dos Arroyos* (two rivers). There was nothing at any of these named spots in the jungle, he said. The geologists of Union Oil had used many of them as camp sites, and he would recognize them when he reached them. He said we were heading now for another *corozal* where there was *cambo* to eat. It was only halfway to Dos Arroyos, and no water would be found in between.

Pablo said at the rate we were going, we wouldn't make El Arbolito for a week. He called the trail we had cut with Carmen *El Camino Abierto*, the open trail. It had ended just beyond El Arbolito.

Then he said, "*Estas flojo, no aguanta*" (You're weak, you won't make it). I told him I hadn't slowed us down yet, and that I would last as long as he did. He smiled slightly and said that *gringos* just don't last in the jungle. I said I was no *gringo*, I was Italian. Wasn't I born in *los Estados Unidos?* he asked. Yes, I said. Then, he said, you are *gringo*. I said no; as far as I was concerned a *gringo* was a Northern European and an Italian was a Latin. Pablo seemed confused then, but I didn't realize why until a few days later. For the moment, I let the whole thing drop. We had enough troubles.

A few minutes later we started out on the trail again and then, abruptly, it disappeared. It took Pablo almost a half hour to find it. It was becoming disheartening, losing all this precious time, but most of all there was the fear of getting lost. I usually stayed ten feet behind Pablo on the trail. At one point I spotted his knife on the ground, picked it up and handed it to him. He couldn't understand how he had dropped it and I couldn't understand how he could be so careless with something that could mean life or death to us. Not wanting to antagonize him, however, I said nothing.

By two P.M. we reached the *corozal* Pablo had mentioned and decided to stop for the day. He wanted to hunt for *cambo* and I wanted to see if I could cut off the ends of the carved stones I was carrying to lighten my load a bit.

I started cutting immediately, using the blade of my Swiss army knife, while Pablo went off hunting for *cambo*. Limestone is not granite, but nevertheless it is stone and this southern Peten brand was like marble. It was rough going but I persisted. After an hour I had only cut a quarter-inch ridge around the largest piece.

Pablo had returned about that time with seven *cambo*. It was our first positive luck all day and it brightened things up considerably. I kept working on the stones while Pablo built the *champa* and slung the hammocks. After another hour I broke the large stone I was working on. Luckily the smallest piece had most of the glyph carving on it, so I decided to keep it and leave the other piece behind. But that put an end to my cutting. I didn't want to ruin any of the other pieces.

Pablo had a fire going and was cooking the *cambo*, and while he waited, I wrote a bit in my notebook. With all the backtracking we had done, I estimated our forward progress at a scant eight kilometers or five miles. Pablo had already estimated the distance from Poptún to the ruins at forty *leguas*—160 kilometers or 100 miles. We had gone only twenty kilometers in two days, and at this rate it would take us another fourteen days! It was a hopeless prospect.

When I gave Pablo the figures he was appalled. He said the trail was impossible. He couldn't understand how such a wide trail had grown over in two years. The trail was *torcido* and *Dios* must be punishing us for something. The whole trip had been *torcido* from the start and he was crazy to have come in the first place.

I listened to his tirade in silence and then said a few words in consolation. He would have none of it. He bellowed that the trail was impossible and he should take off and leave me. I was holding him back!

At this I lost my temper. I said I knew and he knew that I was not slowing us down, and we both knew that if anything was slowing us down it was the damned grown-in trail, the one *he* kept losing.

He cursed and said I was weak and no one else would have stayed with me in such a situation. Carmen wouldn't have, if he were with me, he said.

I told him I knew damn well he had left me that morning, and the only reason he had returned was because he was afraid to go on alone. Then he made the slip.

He shouted that he, Pablo Paredes, was not afraid of any jungle, but only of explaining why he had returned without me back in Poptún. The cat was out of the bag! I stared him dead in the eyes, watching his expression change as he realized what he had said. The strain of the ordeal was beginning to show, and we had both lost our tempers unreasonably. Deciding to drop the argument right there I changed the subject, I asked if the *cambo* was done. Pablo raked at the fire and threw me two. I pulled a Nu-V bar out of my pack, split it, and handed half to Pablo. We ate without speaking.

Darkness fell and finally I broke the mood by saying we only had half a canteen of water left. Pablo said there might be an arroyo with water two *leguas* ahead on the trail—if there was a trail, and if there was water, he added bitterly. We were at the height of the rainy season, and now suddenly, for three days straight, it hadn't rained a drop.

It was only six o'clock but our worry and tension, topped off by our argument, drove us into our hammocks. For the moment we had nothing more to say to each other.

I lay there full of aches and pains. I was physically beat and mentally dazed. Already I noticed a feeling of lightness in my head, due to lack of food. Already the impossible trail, as Pablo called it, had caused an irreparable rift in our relationship. And only two days out from the ruins! With luck and determination we could double our speed, but it still left seven full days ahead. And what if the trail continued on as badly overgrown as it had been? Could we possibly endure fourteen days of such a pace without food? It seemed doubtful. Our only medicine now consisted of a small vial of sulfa powder for cuts, an almost empty tube of Ben Gay, and a few vitamin C tablets. Exhausted and unable to think clearly any longer, I fell asleep.

2 · SPINES AND VINES

BY SEVEN O'CLOCK the next morning we were on the trail again. It was no better than the day before, but feeling better after the night's rest we forged ahead with new energy and determination.

When I had gotten up that morning, I noticed that the *arrador* bites I had received on my shins had gotten infected and were festering. It was small wonder: although the bites on other parts of my body had healed, my lower legs were constantly being entangled and scraped with vines, rapped by branches and punctured by spines. I had put sulphur powder on a few spots, and now noticed that the vines seemed to be getting thicker on the trail and the spine trees more numerous. So at the beginning of our third day out from the ruins, another misfortune was added to my burden. Leg infections and the threat of gangrene.

To add to my misery, I also had a dozen *zancudo* bites on my body. These large mosquitoes can bite through anything, even leather, and their sting swells to a hard lump and itches for days. These bites also fester and infect easily.

As a brief respite, from our troubles, we came upon a small mound of cut limestone blocks, the ruin of a small temple. Pablo said he had never noticed it before. I asked if we were on the right trail. He said, *"Mas o menos"* (more or less), but that he was now using the compass as much as the trail. I checked many of the stones to see if they were carved, but found none, and we continued on.

By eight-thirty we lost the trail completely. Pablo, not bothering to find it, set a new compass course and I saw him constantly looking up at the tall trees above for some he might recognize. We went on through the tangle as best we could, stooping under limbs, sidestepping others, and in places literally pushing our way through walls of underbrush. We took an awful beating, and the *bejucos* (vines) were a particular hindrance. They seemed to grab at my legs and pull like living hands of steel, and my shin scabs broke open and began to bleed.

Pablo was in the lead with compass and knife, but my Swiss-army knife was of little use against the tangle of vines. By ten o'clock we took the last few swallows of water from the canteen. Awhile later Pablo found a *cambo*, and we ate it raw.

By now the temperature had climbed to the mid-eighties, and struggling through the trailless maze had us sweat-soaked and tired. We pushed on, and time after time I became ensnared in the vines and cursed them out loud. The spines were also ripping our clothing, and occasionally I took one in the hand or foot.

I asked Pablo why there were so many vines and spines. He said, "*La selva es asi,*" the jungle is like that. Every place in it has something special, and this particular area ran for many *leguas* with mostly spine trees and many vines.

Unlike me, the man of iron seldom complained about *mi selva,* his jungle, as he called it. He accepted it passively, as a fact of life.

The ancient Mayan civilization has left its mark on its descendants. Even today the Mayan-Spanish Indians, such as Pablo, have a stoic, fatalistic attitude about them. I have never heard a baby cry in Guatemala. Neither do these people laugh. A broad, smiling chuckle is the closest they come to it.

Shortly before noon we reached the arroyo, with a great relief. It was almost dry, with a few inches of water in long puddles here and there, but it looked great. As thirsty as we were, I filled my canteen and put several halazone tablets in. We waited only fifteen minutes instead of the usual half hour before we drank. Then we started off again toward Dos Arroyos, by compass.

We continued through a maze of leaves and branches, Pablo constantly checking his compass, until an hour later we reached what Pablo called a *pinal* (a pine grove, actually, but he was using it to mean spine grove). A pine needle has much the same appearance as most of the hard, sharp spines in the jungle, the *chapai* spines especially.

At any rate, this "*pinal*" was a thick mass of three-to five-foot-tall tropical plants, which resembled the Mexican *maguey* from which tequila is made. These, however, had one-inch hooked barbs along the edge of each of its spreading leaves, which branched up from a central core near the ground and then fell out in a drooping effect. To add to the difficulty of getting through this madness, which lay on either side as far as we could see, it was dotted with trees hung with vines.

Pablo said there was no use trying to go around it, as we might go completely off course, so we started cautiously through. The hooked barbs tore at our clothes, ripping through them and into our bare skin. After a hundred meters, we were torn and bleeding. My shins had been ripped in several places and I had three gashes in my right hand. Then, to our relief, the *pinal* began to thin out enough for us to pass between the savage plants, and after awhile they disappeared completely.

I stopped and put sulphur powder on the worst of our wounds, and we kept going through the now seemingly more friendly maze of trees and vines. Still it was tough going. Awhile later we stopped for a breather and split another Nu-V bar. These bars never failed to restore our energy quickly, but now they were almost gone; and with them, the end of our food supply.

Lying back against my pack, I dozed off. I woke up into a dreamlike disorientation and for several seconds had no idea where I was or why. But I quickly recovered my senses, and realized with a sudden shock exactly where I was and the spot I was in.

Pablo said I had only slept for ten minutes but it was best that we start out again. Getting to my feet I felt dizzy, but after a few minutes of following Pablo through the jungle, I regained what strength, I still had.

Pablo kept saying we wouldn't make Dos Arroyos today. He was completely disheartened at how badly the trail had grown in, and although we came across a stretch of it now and then, he was relying mainly on his compass and his recognition of landmark trees and places. I kept telling him that we must, at all costs, reach Dos Arroyos before dark. He was doubtful.

Without warning we ran across the trail again, and miraculously it was open, with a two-foot cleavage between the branches. To us it looked like a highway. Our spirits lightened and we walked along it at a fast pace. An hour later, at two-thirty in the afternoon, we reached a clear area of the jungle.

Pablo stopped, unslung his pack and, slumping to the ground, announced our arrival at Dos Arroyos. I could hardly believe it. I joined Pablo on the ground to rest, and we had a pipeful of tobacco.

I lay there looking up through the treetops. After awhile Pablo went off to search for *cambo,* and I sat up to write my daily notes. The jungle around me was sparsely treed and I could easily see a hundred feet in all directions. After awhile the sun came out and broke through the foliage, a few sunbeams actually managing to reach the ground. It was beautiful, and with the prospect of a clear trail ahead I felt reborn.

Pablo returned with both *cambo* and *pacaia* shoots and I felt even better. There was plenty of dry wood around, and I must have gathered a hundred pounds while Pablo built a *champa* and slung the hammocks. Then we cooked the *cambo* and *pacaia* and also ate a quarter of a Nu-V bar for nutrients. The *pacaia* has vitamins but the *cambo* is only a stomach filler. We built a huge fire and sat around it.

As we talked, I got on the subject of Pablo's having been a *chiclero.* These men hunt out the *chico sapote,* or chicle gum tree, to drain its sap, from which chewing gum is made. I asked Pablo how it was done.

A good chico sapote is hard to find, he began. If it is too young, it is useless to bother with. If it is too old, it can no longer be tapped. It should be about three or four feet in diameter. I asked how often a tree can be tapped. He said that once a tree has been drained, it cannot be cut again for six to eight years. A large tree yields five to twelve pounds of chicle, a smaller one from three to five pounds.

The *chiclero* climbs twenty feet up the trunk with the aid of spiked shoes and rope, like a lumberjack topper, and begins his cuts. These cuts are called *sangrias*. Each is two feet long, diagonally made, and intersects the middle of the next lower cut. He continues cutting down for fifteen feet until he reaches four or five feet above ground level. There he knocks in a peg at the bottom cut for the white sticky fluid to drip off, and ties a *bolsa*, or bag, below it to catch it. It takes several hours for the bag to fill with *resina*, the raw chicle fluid.

Once ready, it must be boiled in a large pot for two and a half to three hours, with continual stirring. When it reaches a cream color and a certain consistency, and all the water has boiled out, it is ready to cool. Pablo said some *chicleros* stick-dip it until a huge ball of dry chicle has formed around the stick. But, he said, the best way was to pour it into *madera* (wood) molds which have been rubbed with soap, so the chicle won't stick. These molds hold twenty to twenty-five pounds of chicle. I asked Pablo how much he was paid for these *marquetas*, as he called the molds. He smiled and said that the price varied according to the season and the buyer, and especially how good the chicle was. Maybe four or five *quezales* was an average price. I told him it wasn't much for all that work, but Pablo thought it was quite fair. After thinking about the low price of chewing gum and comparing weight to cost, I had to agree with him. At eight o'clock we turned in for the night, tired but with new hope for the trail ahead.

We were up at daybreak the following morning. By seven o'clock we had broken camp and were saying good-by to the clearing called Dos Arroyos. I had asked Pablo the night before where the two arroyos were and he had said there was only one small one. He had gotten the water from it and I had never even seen it. So how did the place get the name of two arroyos? Pablo didn't know.

The trail that morning was as clear as it had been the day before on the last stretch. We were hoping it would keep up, but it didn't. It kept growing in and disappearing, but Pablo always managed to find it again. Farther along we reached a *tall* cerro and had to skirt along its steep middle. We were getting weaker every day now and it was beginning to slow us down. After we passed the *cerro* we rested and split a Nu-V bar.

Later we reached another *cerro* and had to go right across its top. Again we had to rest. We had a smoke and continued. The spines and vines began to get thick and were becoming a hindrance again. By midmorning we were forced by lack of energy to take our third ten-minute break. On this one, as we lay quietly resting on the ground, Pablo heard something in the trees nearby. He said it was a bird, and taking my pistol, started out after it. A few minutes later I heard two well-spaced shots.

I made my way to Pablo, who was smiling and said he had wounded a *faisano*, but it wouldn't fall. He pointed it out, about fifty feet up on a branch. We had to decide whether to chance our last remaining shot on the bird or not. I elected to wait fifteen minutes to see if it would fall. It flew to several branches, and after fifteen minutes I decided to bring it down. I fired and the bird flew to another branch. Pablo swore he had hit it at least once with the first two shots. I knew I had clipped it with the last shot, as a few feathers drifted down, but the big bird refused to fall and die. We kept hoping it would, but after a half hour we gave up, when it flew off, branch by branch, and disappeared in the treetops. Now our ammunition was gone, and with it our last hope of adding to our now almost non-existent food supply.

We went on, the thought of missing the *faisano* and using

up our last rounds annoying us. To add to our worries, we only had one quart of water left in my canteen. Pablo said we would find no water until we reached *La Cuchara,* our next jungle clearing. That was twenty kilometers ahead. To top off the bleak situation, the trail began to disappear again and Pablo started checking his compass. Then, just before noon, he lost it completely.

While he went to search for signs of the trail, it started to rain but stopped after fifteen minutes. I sat down and smoked a pinch of tobacco in the pipe. The tobacco was almost gone, and I had only three cigarettes left. I checked the food again. Five Nu-V bars and one can of pemmican remained. According to Pablo's estimate of the distance we had to go, and what I estimated we had already gone, that left us about 110 kilometers (sixty-nine miles) from Poptún.

When Pablo failed to show up after almost an hour, I was again in the clutches of fear and anxiety. I was wondering if he had really abandoned me this time, but after awhile he showed up. He said he had found the trail but it kept disappearing.

We started out again and soon reached an area of particularly spiny trees, hung thick with vines. After another half hour we lost the trail again completely, and in such an area Pablo said it was useless to try to find it or to go on. He then said he didn't think this was the right trail. I asked him if we were lost. Without answering, he started back and we must have backtracked at least two kilometers before he stopped.

I was dejected and beat. On the last kilometer we had cut off and plunged through a four-foot jungle in search of the trail. While Pablo went off again on one of his now normal trail searches, I tried to forget the whole situation. I distracted myself by trimming my moustache, oiling the pistol and finally just lying back on my pack and looking up at the trees. The mosquitoes were feasting on me but I didn't even brush them away. They were little bother compared to my present situation. In fact, I thought of them as company at the time!

Pablo didn't return for almost another hour. This time what he had to say was a shock. There was no sign of a trail *anywhere*. He would have to backtrack by compass another kilometer, he said, and then try a stroke to the north. Again he took off and again I waited. I had to admire the man's spunk, but he had no choice. Now it was do or die; literally.

To distract myself again, I listened intently to the jungle sounds around me. A variety of birds called back and forth to each other. Most of them seemed to be in the lower branches of the trees, but a few macaw shrieks could be heard up in the high overhead canopy of the jungle giants. Odd cricket-type sounds were everywhere. I estimated the temperature at ninety degrees, and it was humid.

Forty-five minutes later, at three P.M. Pablo returned with good news. He had found the trail and also a good camp site with water. I followed him back in a westerly direction and then we swung north.

Going along, we crossed a line of *zompopo* (leaf cutter) ants, carrying the bright bits of green leaves they had cut over their bodies, as they filed along on the ground. For a brief moment they broke my mood of loneliness. They were like other beings, and like Pablo and I intent in their mission. We stopped for a minute to watch them. It was a curious sight to see them going along the jungle floor, so orderly, paying no attention to us. Their cargo kept bobbing from side to side above them, as if they were waving large green fans. We stepped over them and continued on.

A half hour later we reached a *corozal*. Pablo said this was the spot and we stopped. He showed me a dried-up arroyo with a few inches of stale water running for a few feet through it.

Pablo built our nightly *champa* and we slung our hammocks. He said there were no *cambos* in these corozo palms. They were too old. The *cambo* is the heart of the sapling coroso, lying a foot below where the fronds begin to grow out of the trunk. There was nothing to do but open our last can of pemmican. At this point it tasted better than steak, and we ate slowly, savoring each mouthful.

Pablo later pulled out some *tusa* (cornhusk) he had and began to roll a little tobacco in it. This cigarette, which he called a *chencha*, made the strong homegrown tobacco Pablo had stronger than ever, but we passed it back and forth, inhaling deeply and enjoying it to the last puff. It made me dizzy and I asked Pablo if he had anything like marijuana in it. "*Cierto que no!*" (Certainly not!) he said. Then he added that he only had a little something for taste in it. I couldn't get him to identify it, but whatever it was I was happy and carefree. I just sat enjoying the scenery while Pablo gathered wood and started the fire.

Later I decided to see what I could do with my sandals. They had been slipping badly, and for two days I had been walking on my heels and toes. They were full of spines and ached so much I had forgotten my festering shins. I found that there were large scabs of running sores from my heels to my ankles. I doctored them the best I could with the sulphur powder, and then sewed my sandals with extra *pita* cloth.

Pablo hadn't been able to get the fire started, so I gave it a try. He said it was useless but after an hour I got it going. I used dead coroso leaves to start it. Pablo said I was just lucky. I said no, just Italian.

Awhile later it started to rain so we got into our hammocks and went to sleep. The rain continued off and on all night and between it, my aching heels and shins and the dampness of the night, I woke up several times.

Around three in the morning I was soaking wet. The rain had dripped in off my hammock cover. My left shin was now throbbing with pain. Not wanting to use up the only flashlight we had, as it was getting dimmer every night, I put more sulphur powder on my leg and bound it with the last of my bandages, all in the dark. I lay there wet, cold, hungry and tired, too uncomfortable to sleep. The rain began to come down heavier than ever. After what seemed like an eternity, I dozed off. It was already getting light.

At six o'clock we got up, split a Nu-V bar, broke camp and started out on the trail an hour later. In ten minutes we lost it again and Pablo started using his compass, heading east-northeast and checking it every thirty feet or so. After an hour, Pablo got worried with the erratic readings he was getting and took off again to search for the trail.

I noticed a fairly clear spot with some limestone rocks nearby, and went to sit on them. The bandage on my leg was loose and I began to fix it. My leg was getting worse, so I put a few more pinches of sulphur powder on it. After I had finished, it struck me that one of the rocks appeared to be a cut block. . . . It was!

Looking around, I found I was sitting on a small mound of cut stones. Another sign of a ruin nearby, I thought. Or was the whole area just an extension of Machaquilá, now fifty-six kilometers, thirty miles, behind us? If so, it would make it by far the largest ruin site in all of Mayadom. But this will not be known until a large team of archeologists combs the area, which probably will not happen for fifty years or more, as there are many other sites of seemingly greater interest to investigate first. Until then the matter is open to speculation.

Sometime later Pablo returned. He had found the trail and I followed him to it. At times it was quite clear and then it would grow together again. We lost it and found it twice and then began to encounter *tapóns* of trees across its path. It was dangerous to go around them as we might lose the trail, and going through them was almost impossible. More often than not we made our way through, the branches interlaced with almost impenetrable vines, the spine trees frequent enough to inflict more painful barbs into our already weak and pain wracked bodies. Pablo again kept remarking how incredible it was that a trail as wide as three meters had grown in after two years.

Occasionally Pablo would look back and see me struggling and ask if I was OK. I would answer him with "*Yo te seugo*" (I follow you) and occasionally he would say that he had been praying to *primero Dios y La Virgen*. He felt it was helping so all I said was "*Bueno.*" After an hour we had gone through or around a dozen or more *tapóns* and we were exhausted and disgusted.

But there was no rest for the weary; we soon encountered a *cerro*, then another and another. We had to go over all of them as the trail was still visible in spots along them. They were not high but in our condition any incline was almost too much to face. My back ached from the frame on my pack's digging into me. My legs were sore, inflamed and aching, and my hands and feet burned and throbbed from the many spines in them. We were both weak from lack of food but we went on and on. It began to seem endless and hopeless, and my head reeled dizzily. I noticed a few cut stones on one of the *cerros*, but didn't even stop to examine them, I was so desperate with exhaustion.

Pablo was like a madman, crashing ahead through the thick jungle and I had told myself I would keep up with his pace. Somehow I did, and by eleven o'clock, after a terrible three-hour forced march, without a break, we stumbled into the clearing known as *La Cuchara*.

Without a word we sank to the ground, panting. We must have lain there for fifteen minutes before I sat up, feeling somewhat dizzy but much better. I asked Pablo why this place

was called The Spoon. He said it was where one of the Union
Oil geologists had lost one. I had to smile at that.

We sat there awhile longer and then left again on the trail
for El Presidente, which Pablo said was the next spot and only
two *leguas* away. This place was so named because it was another of the geologists' camps, and they were there when they
heard of the assassination of the Guatemalan President, Cas-
tillo Armas (July 26, 1957).

We weren't on the trail five minutes when it started to
rain like mad, but we continued on in the downpour. I put on
my poncho, but I soon noticed that Pablo's thin shirt was torn
to shreds and sticking like strips of wet cloth to his half naked
body. I took off my fatigue jacket and gave it to him, putting
my poncho on again over my khaki shirt. The fatigue jacket
wasn't water proof, but it would at least keep the spines from
ripping his skin. Anyway his shirt was now of no use and he
would need something to keep him warm at night.

The downpour continued for an hour, then ended as
quickly as it had started. The trail was fairly clear in spots
now, and we went ahead at a good pace through the wet
leaves. But our speed and energy were soon cut short by a 500-
foot *cerro*, over which the trail led. It was steep and slippery,
with wet, loose limestone rocks, and it was a struggle to gain
the top. We made it; then decending it, we ran into three
smaller ones beyond.

By the time we were going down the last one I was again
weak and dizzy, but not far beyond it Pablo announced our
arrival at El Presidente. It was two P.M. and we had gone sixteen kilometers. I decided that was enough for the day. We
were both dead tired.

The arroyo nearby was dry, but we decided to camp there
overnight anyway. After a short rest Pablo started to build a
champa and I gathered some wood. It was wet and I took an

hour to get a fire started. When the hammocks were slung, we finally relaxed for the night and split a Nu-V bar for supper. I could have eaten two whole ones myself, but that was exactly what we had left now. Two Nu-V bars. And we weren't even at the halfway mark back to Poptún!

However, the situation wasn't hopeless. Pablo said if the trail held up as it had for the last eight kilometers, since La Cuchara, we could make the open trail we had cut with Carmen and the mule at El Arbolito, in two days. From there it was another forty kilometers or three more days on the open trail to Concomá, food and salvation. The question was now an equation between sixty-odd kilometers, our diminishing energy and two Nu-V bars, totaling 400 calories.

To add to my problems, my left leg was beginning to swell and both my hands and feet were already swollen and aching with their burden of festering spine points. To lower our dropping morale, further, we smoked our last cigarette that night. A regular Chesterfield.

As we smoked, we got into a conversation on geography. Pablo asked me how big the United States was. I told him that it was 5000 kilometers between the Atlantic and Pacific oceans. He thought that was incredible. Then I mentioned something about South America. When I told him how large it was, he was again amazed; he only knew of three countries in the whole continent.

The conversation drifted into history and I mentioned Napoleon. Pablo had never heard of him. I said he was an emperor of France 150 years ago. Pablo had not heard of France. I said it was in Europe. Pablo's face was a blank. He had never heard of Europe. After a few more comments I realized that he knew hardly anything of geography or history. Now I understood why he had been confused when I had said that I was not a *gringo*, but an Italian. He had, of course, never heard of Italy either. I gave him a brief geography lesson, which seemed to confuse him, so after awhile I dropped the whole thing. We dried our clothes by the fire and at eight o'clock went to bed.

I was awakened at ten by rain and found myself once again soaking wet in my hammock. I had been sleeping with my poncho on as it was too cold without it, but I was wet from the waist down. Pablo still had his blanket and wasn't bothered too much by the cold nights. Furthermore, I always slung my hammock on the outside of the *champa*, so Pablo could stay dry in the middle. His hammock had no cover over it, but mine was becoming useless.

It was a cold, miserable night for me, and between that and thinking about our chances of getting out of the jungle alive I slept very little, dozing off only to wake up again, wet, shivering and depressed.

3 · LOST IN THE JUNGLE

AT DAWN I got up and started the fire to try to get some of the chill out of my bones, but it didn't help much. When Pablo got up we broke camp, had a quarter of a Nu-V bar each, and started out on the trail. The day was Monday, the seventh of December. Before we left I had jotted in my notebook that it was the twenty-third anniversary of Pearl Harbor. I had no idea at the time that it was an ominous warning. In fact, at first the day started out great.

The trail was in fair shape and we encountered no *tapóns* the first hour. We even found and ate a cambo raw. It was sour and hard on our stomachs but for awhile it stopped the gnawing ache of hunger. Then the day began to take shape.

Pablo lost the trail and it took him a half hour to find it.

By ten o'clock we reached a tremendous *tapón* between two *cerros*. That steep, tree-strewn gorge looked impassable, but Pablo said it was the only way. The trail lay somewhere through it, he said, and we must follow it no matter what. I asked him if this *tapón* was familiar to him. He said it wasn't but that it could easily have fallen in the last two years. We started up through it.

Our weakness now became painfully evident. As we went through the tangle of limbs and over and under the huge tree trunks, we began to move in slow motion. Obstacles which would have been easily overcome normally now seemed almost impossible. My twenty-five-pound pack, my infected leg, my spine-filled hands and feet and my spinning head, all told me that the climb across the *cerros* was impossible, not to mention the unending trees across the steep ravine.

Still Pablo slowly made his way through and continued to climb higher and higher, up through the fallen debris, and in a supreme effort of will power I made my pain-wracked, exhausted body follow him. It was a nightmare in which I knew I could not stop and which appeared always the same and endless.

After nearly an hour we gained the summit and, exhausted, fell to rest. I asked Pablo how many fallen trees we had encountered on our way up and he said maybe twenty-five or thirty. I decided to split a quarter piece of Nu-V bar with Pablo, for a small boost of energy. It worked. Awhile later I wearily got to my feet and we started down the other side of the saddle between the *cerros*.

This time it was downhill and luckily only a half dozen fallen trees lay in our path. The trail was no longer visible but Pablo, going by compass, said he knew we were heading in the right direction and even spotted a few familiar places in the area. Then we came upon a small grove of *pacaia* shoots, finding twenty in all. Farther on we hit a swampy area, but it wasn't as bad as the one we had gone through a few days before. However, it did slow us down and sapped more of our energy than the distance we splashed through it warranted.

On the other side of the swamp the trees thinned out considerably and we could see ahead through the jungle quite a way. I began to get a strange feeling about the place and started to put the pieces together. Pablo had not remembered seeing the great *tapón* of trees between the *cerros* before. Even the *cerros* had been somewhat unfamiliar to him. Moreover, beyond them, we had found no trail and we were now moving along by compass alone. In my dazed condition I was blindly following Pablo, depending solely on his judgment. But even an old jungle-wise *chiclero* was not infallible, I thought, and he too was weak and confused.

I asked Pablo if he was sure we were heading in the right direction and he said yes, he had been reading the compass every fifteen meters. I didn't want to ask to check it but I made a point of telling him to keep a close check on it. He replied angrily that he was perfectly capable of reading a compass.

We continued through the now sparsely treed undergrowth. Soon up ahead through the treetops we spotted a high ridge. Pablo said he recognized it and there was a pass through it, but I still had the odd feeling that this was *not* the right direction. Some fifteen minutes later we reached the base of the ridge. Going along it, Pablo said this was not the ridge he knew, as he could not find the pass through it. He had never seen it before.

A flash of terror swept over me. I took the compass from Pablo and couldn't believe what it read. Instead of northeast we had been heading in the *opposite* direction! I jiggled the compass and read it again. Same reading, southwest. Pablo was completely at a loss to explain it. I suggested that in his weakened condition it was an easy mistake to read south for north. He insisted he hadn't, but there was no other explanation.

With a fear now upon us, we headed back, retracing our steps as fast as we could. My head was light and I felt dizzy, but the prospect of being lost had obviously started the adrenalin moving in my system, and I felt stronger than I had in days. We soon reached the swamp and splashed quickly through it. Then we were attacked by falling ants from the trees above us and several got down our necks. We had to strip almost naked to get rid of them.

But we had more serious things on our minds. Pablo couldn't get over having made such a deadly mistake. The situation was black but I tried to repair Pablo's broken confidence in himself; anyone could have made such a mistake, I told him. The point now was to find the right trail and save our lives.

We backtracked about four kilometers, right through the great *tapón*, and when that was accomplished, we were fully exhausted and a great fear was swelling within us. Pablo looked as if he had seen a ghost, and his apparent confusion didn't help my feelings at all. If the great jungle tracker, my man of iron, was lost and bewildered I had good cause for alarm.

My fear grew as we stumbled on. Finally at two o'clock Pablo folded for the day. He said he couldn't go on. I was surprised and alarmed, but I was beat myself and didn't argue.

We sat in the middle of the thick jungle in silence for a few minutes, resting. Then Pablo said he wouldn't make a *champa* that night, as there were no guano or corozo palms around. I insisted we must. As if to prove my point it started to rain.

I found a small grove of five-foot long *platanio* leaves, but Pablo said the rain would only tear them to shreds. I insisted he make a *champa* with them anyway and in the now heavy downpour I helped him with it. When it was done we found some wood, but the fire wouldn't start. Pablo gave up on the wet wood after an hour, but I refused to and continued on. Two hours later I too gave up. We would have no fire that night.

Darkness had fallen and the rain continued in a tremendous downpour all night. The *platanio* leaves were soon torn to shreds and we laid in our hammocks soaking wet, trying to sleep. The day had been cold, not hitting seventy degrees, I thought, but now the temperature dropped down to the low fifties. It was a cold, wet, hungry night and we were full of fear and dread of what lay ahead of us. We were lost in the jungle, weak and without food, and I was getting feverish, with my left leg worse than ever.

By midnight I was intolerably cold and hungry. For an hour I tried to warm my wet and frozen feet with the cigarette lighter, holding the flame directly under them. I felt nothing but an occasional burn on my skin. My feet were numb and I was shivering so hard I thought I would shake apart.

Then the lighter fluid gave out. Luckily Pablo's lighter was still working, otherwise we would have been in a bad way. I began to rub my feet and arms and legs, but after awhile I lay back in my misery and dozed off from exhaustion. But the haunting dread of knowing we were lost in the jungle brought me fearfully awake several times during the night.

The rain continued until almost daybreak, when we both got up. Pablo had spent a fairly warm and dry night in his blanket and hammock, which he had slung under mine. He went off into the jungle and after a half hour he came back with a *cambo*. We ate it raw, then split our last one-third of a Nu-V bar. *Now all our food was gone.*

By seven we were ready to go and started out by compass in a northeasterly direction. Pablo kept saying he didn't think we had passed this way yesterday, but I pointed out things that indicated we had. The sky was overcast and there was no way of telling by the sun if our compass was correct. Also I was getting worried about Pablo. He seemed to be completely disoriented and demoralized. I suggested I take the lead with the compass but he got angry and said he could do much better than I so I let the matter drop. But I knew we could not afford to lose the trail we were backtracking on. If we didn't reach *La Machaca*, our next jungle clearing, we would perish for lack of food and energy. And I knew we would have to reach it today. By eight-thirty we were both dead tired and suddenly Pablo stopped and said simply that he had lost the trail. Completely crushed, we sat down to think.

Then I noticed the jungle getting lighter around us. The sun had broken through the overcast and I could see it through the high trees above. I checked the compass. It was right! We were still heading in a generally northeast direction, but now we had lost the trail from which we had strayed yesterday. I sat there wondering what our chances were of getting out alive.

Finally Pablo got up and without spirit said he would see if he could find the trail. He left and I was alone, as alone and desperate as I have ever been in my life, weak from hunger and exhaustion, aching all over from spines festering in my skin. I used the last bit of sulphur powder on my legs and sat there in fear.

With death staring me in the face, life seemed simple now and beautiful. Gone were my aspirations for fame and fortune. I would have settled gladly for the existence of a farmer's daily struggle in the fields, if only I could live. Could it all end like this? I, a city dweller, dying out here in the middle of the jungle? I refused to believe it, and all the while I knew it was true. There I was, sitting in the middle of nowhere, beaten down by infection and exhaustion and wasting away with malnutrition. Lost in a jungle, fifty miles from the nearest village.

Suddenly it all became so real I was deafened by a thunderous silence. My mind seemed to comprehend all the unknown mysteries of the universe at once, and I realized, as in an awakening from a dream, that there were none. The greatest mystic's mysteries were nothing more than unrealistic dreams. It was all a search for reality. . . . And I suddenly said to myself, sitting there on the jungle floor, that I would not die. Not here and now, I said. Not like this. I'll make it if I have to crawl.

My thoughts were interrupted by Pablo returning through the undergrowth. The look on his face took the edge off my pledge of courage. He said gravely that no trail of any kind could be seen anywhere. For the first time he admitted we were lost, and his words fell on me like continuing deathly echoes: *Estamos perdidos . . . Estamos perdidos.*

I stood up shakily. We had both known for twenty-four hours that we were lost in the jungle. But this was the first time that either of us had actually stated it as a fact. I saw the fear in Pablo's eyes and I knew he saw mine.

Without a word we started out by compass in a northeast direction once more, not knowing if we would ever find the trail again or what fate lay before us in the wilderness. We only knew we had to keep walking. If we walked far enough we were bound to reach somewhere. The question was, could we last?

We continued silent for awhile and finally Pablo spoke. He said that even if we didn't find the trail, in the direction we were now heading we were bound to hit the Rio Machaquilá. I knew that too, but I also knew it would take us two or three extra days to reach the open trail along the Rio—*if* we could find it along the Rio. I didn't mention it to Pablo. I knew that he knew it too. There was nothing to say or do, except keep walking.

Exhausted, I was stumbling along in a half stupor, know-

ing that we might never make it out alive, and yet our desperate situation was the one thing that kept me going at that
point. I kept thinking, if we can keep moving we might make
it.

Then after ten o'clock, we came upon a trail. Pablo
thought it was the right one. According to the compass it was
headed in the general direction of La Machaca. After an hour
Pablo said he had spotted a familiar area and was sure this was
the right trail, but after the previous day I still had my doubts.

When we had been on the wrong trail for hours the day
before, he had said the same thing. Later, as we backtracked,
he hadn't even spotted some places that I recognized from
only a few hours before. How could I be sure he had now seen
and remembered a place on the trail after two years? It wasn't
logical and I couldn't accept his assured reply that this *was* the
right trail, but I said nothing. I was hoping it was myself, and
besides I didn't want to shake Pablo's confidence again.
Whatever trail we were on, it was headed in as good a direction as we could have set by compass. Silently I stumbled on
behind Pablo, exhausted and aching, hoping for the best.

Then the trail began to grow in, at times virtually disappearing, and we were beset by all kinds of obstacles. The vines
and spine trees began to thicken again and we fought to free
ourselves, our clothes getting torn almost to shreds. My
poncho was in tatters. Then we ran into a swamp. Pablo insisted that this was the right trail and we had to follow it
through the swamp. It turned out to be as bad as the worst we
had come upon. At times the water was so deep we had to
swim. Luckily it was only a depression between two *cerros* that
had filled with water, and after a hundred yards we were
through it.

We were both now going on will power alone. Pablo
looked so thin and haggard I didn't understand what was holding him up. I wondered what *I* looked like. I felt I must soon

die from exhaustion. We rested for ten minutes and went on. Ahead lay a large *cerro*, which we ended up climbing. I couldn't understand how I made the steep incline, but after a terrible struggle, at times down on all fours, I reached the top right behind Pablo. We fell down sprawling and rested for fifteen minutes.

After we descended, a whole series of *cerros* and rocky passes began. They were not high, but all were dangerously strewn with loose stones and holes and thicketed with spine trees. It was one of the worst spots of the whole return trip, and I was afraid I'd break an ankle. If I did, I knew it would be all over for sure. I asked Pablo several times if he was sure this was the right trail. It was, he said, without a doubt.

We crossed the middle of a small *cerro* and saw another huge one ahead. Pablo stopped and excitedly told me that on the other side of that *cerro* lay La Machaca! With a flush of hope and renewed energy, we reached the *cerro* and started up. On the way I slipped to the ground several times and barely made it to my feet. My legs and feet ached dreadfully and I'll never know how I climbed that last *cerro*. My head was in a spinning stupor and my eyes couldn't focus properly. Ahead of me Pablo was not doing much better, but finally in agony we gained the summit.

We decided not to sit down and rest, as we would probably doze off and sleep, so we leaned against trees for awhile and then began to shuffle down the other side of the *cerro*. It was a gradual decline, and soon we stumbled into a large, sparsely wooded area. After another half hour, at two P.M., Pablo announced that we were in the place called La Machaca!

We staggered across a clearing and collapsed by an arroyo. It was a sight. Twenty-five feet wide and full of water. I was tremendously relieved, and having reached this point considered that our lives were saved. We were not lost any more. But

Pablo assumed a serious mood. He reminded me that we were now *only at the halfway mark to Poptún.*

The realization didn't dampen my high spirits. We now had only ten or twelve kilometers between us and the open trail at El Arbolito. From that point there would at least be no danger of getting lost again, I reminded Pablo. "Sí," he said seriously, but added it was sixty kilometers from El Arbolito to the *ranchera* near Concomá.

I insisted we could make it. At the *ranchera* we could boil corn to eat.

I had expected the arrival at La Machaca to brighten Pablo's spirits, but he seemed almost as depressed as ever. It was a foreboding of things to come, but at the time I was so happy not to be lost any more that I didn't give it a second thought.

All I could think was that our lives were saved, and that the terror of the jungle trip was now over. I was too optimistic.

4 · HOPE, HUNGER AND DESPERATION

WE LAY ON the ground at La Machaca and, looking up into the treetops with a reborn feeling, I dozed off into a tranquil sleep.

I awoke sometime later to find Pablo unloading an armful of wood. He asked where I wanted the *champa* built. I picked out a good spot fifteen feet from the arroyo and he started on it. I asked Pablo if there were any fish in the arroyo. He said no but I might find some *jútes* in it. I didn't understand what he meant until he went to the arroyo and brought one back to me. It was a two-inch snail, the same kind I had noticed one day on the Rio Machaquilá.

While he slung the hammocks I took the coffee tin, waded into the arroyo, and began to pick the largest ones off the bottom. The arroyo varied from one to two feet deep, and was as much sharp rock as mud on the bottom. My left heel was badly bruised and full of spines, and I had a rough time, but after an hour I had found about fifty and cleaned out a hundred-foot stretch of the arroyo.

Back at the *champa* Pablo already had the fire going. I picked out thirty of the largest snails and we boiled them in the coffee tin for fifteen minutes. Then with a hungry zest we began to break off the ends and suck the precious meat out of them. They were tough and flavorless but we enjoyed them, knowing that the energy they would give us might well save our lives. Night had fallen when we had finished, and exhausted from the day's march, we got into our hammocks and dozed off.

I was awakened by a splashing sound in the arroyo. Reaching for my pistol, I realized it was now empty, and useless. I whispered over to Pablo and found that he too had been awakened. *"Que es?"* I asked. *"Danta,"* he whispered back, and we sadly lamented the fact that we had no ammo. Getting out of our hammocks, we crept silently in the dark toward the arroyo. The night air was cold and damp.

Pablo threw the beam of our fading flashlight toward the sounds of the splashing. A beautiful jungle deer stood in the water of the arroyo near the opposite bank, its eyes glowing in the dim light of the beam. It stood like a statue for a few seconds and then splashed up the bank and disappeared into the jungle.

Pablo cursed our luck. He had expected it to be at the near

bank and had been prepared to pounce upon it with the hunting knife. Unhappily, we returned to our hammocks.

Sometime later I woke up shivering with cold and couldn't get back to sleep. The snails we had eaten lay heavy in my stomach. I got up and started the fire. Then I lay on the ground next to it in my poncho and fell asleep. From time to time I would wake up, stoke the dying fire until I got it blazing again, then doze off to sleep next to its warm heat. It felt good to be warm again, and I refused to think of what might crawl up on me during the night.

That morning I woke up chilled in the first light of dawn. The fire had gone dead so I rekindled it. Then I began to fix my sandals, which were now a mess of mud and tied rope. My left heel was aching badly but I could still walk on it. I had no choice, although from now on every step would be painful. My left leg was still swelling and getting worse, the open sores festering and bleeding.

I had gotten used to the ache of spines in my hands but I managed to squeeze out a few anyway. They hurt worse than ever. I decided to forget everything and began to unsling my hammock and pack it. Pablo was soon up and we ate the last few snails for breakfast.

By seven we were on our way, but Pablo could find no trail at the end of the Machaca clearing toward the east. Rather than go by compass, I elected to wade up the arroyo as Pablo said it would lead us to the open trail.

The water was up to our waists and sometimes it almost reached our chins. The rocks on the bottom were treacherous and cut our feet. We waded along for a kilometer and I decided that before we broke an ankle it would be better to try the land route again.

After searching through an incredibly thick tangle of vines and undergrowth for an hour we found the trail. It revived our spirits, but while in some spots it was fair, in others it was completely overgrown. Six or seven times Pablo lost it, then for an anxious five or ten minutes he would search and again find it.

By eleven we were so weak and hungry I decided to stop while Pablo searched for a *pacaia* or *cambo*. In our weakened condition and with the continual loss of the trail and trouble with the thick vines, we had only covered six kilometers in four hours. Pablo returned, after what seemed like an eternity, with a single *cambo*. We ate the bitter pulp and started out again. By one o'clock we reached the bank of the arroyo, and wading across it began to search for the open trail we had cut with Carmen two weeks before. (Two weeks! It seemed like a lifetime!) After a half-hour search, we crashed through an especially thick tangle of undergrowth and stepped into *El Camino Abierto* (the open trail).

I could hardly believe it. We had traversed a hundred kilometers of dense jungle, without a machete, with inadequate food, and had reached the safety and ease of the open trail.

We sat down in the middle of it and smiled at each other. Some minutes later I got up and said that we'd best get started and make as many kilometers as we could before nightfall. Pablo said he was dead tired and insisted we camp there for the night.

His remark and attitude took me completely by surprise. With no forewarning, he suddenly seemed depressed and completely irrational. I sat down and said we could rest another fifteen minutes, but then we'd have to get started. Pablo lay back on the ground and dozed off. Ten minutes later I told him that we must leave. He sat up and announced that he couldn't go any farther that day. We had an argument and I got him on his feet again only by promising to go first.

I was as exhausted as he and my infections had weakened

me, but reaching the trail had given me new courage. Beat as I was, with my head light and dizzy, unsteady on my feet, I now had great hopes of making it out alive.

Taking the lead (for the first time) I started out at a fast pace, Pablo stumbling along behind me. Occasionally he fell so far behind I had to wait for him, and I couldn't believe it. What had happened to my man of iron, the *hombre de hierro* who had told me I was too weak to make it back?

I slowed my pace but Pablo continued to fall behind. He started to moan and said he was dying of hunger. I kept telling him that we would only go another kilometer, but when we reached that point I would insist on one more. Pablo, without a word, kept stumbling on behind me.

Finally I too began to stumble in exhaustion but I refused to stop. The open trail was of small help. Better than anything out in the jungle, it was still only a hastily cut path in the underbrush that we had made two weeks before. Already it was growing in and the trampled branches were sprouting anew. In some spots I actually had to stop and search, to make sure we were still on it.

I had set my sights on ten kilometers on the trail, but when we had covered eight I just couldn't go any further. It was three P.M. I cut off the trail, found a spot to set up camp and collapsed on the ground. Pablo stumbled in behind me and I heard him fall to the ground and moan before I sank off into unconsciousness.

I woke up confused in semi-darkness, unaware for a few seconds of where I was. I checked my watch. It was after five o'clock. We had slept for two hours and Pablo was still out on the ground. I found some wood and started a fire, then I woke him. He seemed frightened but soon came to his senses.

We sat around the fire and I decided that there was no use trying to build a *champa* in the dark. Besides, we were just too tired. We sat up silently staring into the fire for almost an

hour, then Pablo got up and going over to a *chapai* tree, cut off
a bunch of nuts. We were both so hungry we would have
eaten anything. We managed to break open the nuts but they
were hard as rocks. Pablo, depressed and moaning, wrapped
himself in his blanket and went to sleep on the ground near
the fire.

I took out the coffee tin, got a little water boiling and
dropped in the *chapai* nuts. After a half hour they were still
like stones, even though I had managed to cut them in half. I
tried chewing them and managed to swallow a few mouthfuls
of the hard nuts. Then wrapping myself in my hammock, I
joined Pablo on the ground by the fire. In a matter of seconds
I was asleep.

In my exhaustion I slept right through until seven the next
morning. Pablo was still asleep and I had to shake him hard to
get him up. He cursed and moaned something about dying. I
was so weak and dizzy myself it was an effort to get on my feet.
The *chapai* nuts were a lump in my stomach, or maybe it was
hunger cramps. As there was nothing to eat and no camp to
break, we were ready to go in fifteen minutes.

I told Pablo, who was moaning and seemed to be in another world, that we were about twenty-five kilometers from
the *ranchera* near Concomá, and that if we made it we would
have corn to eat but he said it was impossible to do it. He lay
back on the ground groaning about his weak condition. He
said he would never make it. I said he had to, and he *would*
make it. I packed our packs, put Pablo's on his back and after
a half hour of arguing managed to get him on the trail.

We started out, I in the lead again. It was a tremendous
effort just to stay on our feet and keep walking. I was a mass of
aches and pains and kept worrying that my legs would give out
under me. Behind me Pablo was walking like a zombie, stumbling along, wild-eyed.

The open trail was badly grown in but we had reached it

just in time. If we had been in the trackless tangles of the jungle then, we couldn't have managed more than four or five kilometers a day, and every day we would have gone less and less until finally we would have dropped and been unable to get up. Then the long agonizing death from hunger would have begun.

It was a terrible thought. I imagined a vision of death, a ghostly specter, coming along somewhere behind us on the trail, and to stay ahead of it I shambled along ignoring exhaustion and pain, thinking only that with every step we were getting closer and closer to salvation.

I had decided that we would walk, without a break, until we dropped. I knew that once we stopped we might not get up again for hours, and would probably doze off and sleep the day away.

Travel on the trail at night was impossible, even if we had a good flashlight, which we didn't. Ours was now a dull orange glow and only good for looking inside a pack after dark. It might give out completely any second. But the worst dangers were snakes and *tigres*, both night prowlers. If a *tigre* was surprised on the trail he might well leap at us. If he didn't, he might trail us and get us later from behind. But this was only a possible danger. The snakes were a certain one.

At night dozens of varieties crawled the jungle floor or weaved their way high up through the underbrush. The last are the most dangerous, for if one drops on you, shaken from a branch, or if you run into one face to face it means an agonizing death.

A coral snake for instance, is usually seen on the ground in the daytime. At night, however, it goes up into the branches of low trees. The bite of this beautiful little eighteen-inch colubrid is usually fatal in twenty minutes, if it strikes the victim near the head.

At the time, however, I wasn't really thinking of these

things. I knew that traveling at night through the jungle, trail or no trail, was insane. But what I was planning now was almost as bad. In my drunkenlike stupor and my fear of not getting out of there alive, I had decided to walk twenty-five kilometers without a break. Even for someone in top condition this would have been no small feat, but for us it was impossible. But we *had* so far accomplished the impossible. Half-starved, sick, almost out on our feet, we were still moving ahead. For a minute I had a wondrous flash of conviction and courage and insisted to myself that we must keep going and not stop for a rest. Behind me Pablo began to moan and whine again. I told him we must keep going, but I knew he didn't hear.

We went on like two stumbling sleepwalkers, until after what seemed like an eternity, Pablo blurted out behind me, *"El Corozal! El Corozal!"* Then he fell to his knees and rolled over on the ground. I went back to him and fell beside him. He repeated in a gasping whisper that we had reached the place called El Corozal. My eyes couldn't seem to focus correctly but I managed to check my watch and in disbelief found that it was only nine-fifteen. We had only been on the trail two and a half hours. It seemed like ten.

I tried to stand up, but the weight of my pack flipped my body back to the ground. I was completely beat, but to me Pablo looked even worse, spread-eagled like a dead man on the ground. Then I lost consciousness.

I awoke in a frightened daze. Checking my watch, I was relieved to see we had only slept a half hour. Pablo refused to stir when I shook him. Finally he opened his eyes and I helped him sit up. I said we had to go. Again he said he just couldn't make it any more.

He began to talk of sitting there and dying. All he wanted to do was to go to sleep and die. I said he wasn't quitting and he wasn't going to die. He began to whine. Then, sobering up for a moment, he said he had a plan. I would go ahead and reach Concomá, he said, and there I would send someone back to him with food.

I told him I wasn't going ahead alone because I really didn't know the way, and I'd never make it alone in less than three days. By then, I said, I'd be dying somewhere on the trail. I told him I might even get lost. I said I knew he could make it, but we'd have to stick together.

I had said all this to give Pablo courage to go ahead, but then I realized it was all true. I *didn't* know the way. Several times already I'd had to stop and figure out which way the trail went, it was so overgrown. At that rate it would have taken me at least three or possibly four days to reach Concomá, and as I had told Pablo I'd have been dying on the trail by then. And so would he die, waiting back there in the jungle for help which would never arrive. But if we stayed together he could make sure I stayed on the trail and didn't waste time checking it out.

I repeated these things again to Pablo and he seemed to agree, but still he said he didn't think he could go on. I insisted he could, and told him that if we kept steadily on the trail we would make the cave, where we had spent the second night on the way out, by two o'clock. I said it was about eight kilometers away. He asked me if I was sure. I said it was a liberal estimate and that we might even arrive sooner—I was sure. Pablo said he would try to go on, and a few minutes later I helped him to his feet and we started out.

For awhile the brief rest had alleviated some of my exhaustion, but it wasn't long before I again feared I would drop on the trail, and behind me Pablo was muttering that he couldn't make it. He kept gasping out "Ay, Dios mio" (Oh my God) over and over.

We kept staggering on and soon I began to mutter myself, to try to give Pablo courage to go on and to keep my mind off my own exhaustion. I talked to him about his house and family and how nice it would be to get back to Poptún and soon I was just chattering away in a half delirium, about what I can't remember.

My eyes no longer focused and I kept tripping over twigs and branches. Twice I went sprawling to the ground in headlong dives. Each time I managed to climb to my feet and go on.

The whole thing began to take on a dreamlike horror. I was so weak and dizzy I was barely able to stand up, yet somehow I forced my legs to carry me ahead.

Sometime later Pablo fell down with a groaning shout. Turning, I saw him lying on the trail and went back to help him up. He moaned and refused. It took me awhile to get him started again. I had to pull him onto his feet, but I was so weak we both fell down several times. Finally we were both upright and moving again.

At twelve noon, suddenly and without warning, I came upon the cave. I called back excitedly to Pablo and collapsed in its entrance. He came up staggering like a drunk and fell beside me.

After I regained some strength I told Pablo that this was a great stroke of luck. If we could make the *milpa*, only six kilometers ahead, the *ranchera* was across it and we were saved. There was corn to eat there, I said. I kept urging Pablo to go on and after ten minutes we got to our feet and started off, the thought of the *milpa* and the *ranchera* luring us ahead with hope. Before we left I took some of Pablo's load and put it in my pack.

We plodded on for what I estimated at two kilometers, and I swore to myself that I couldn't go on, but somehow I did. Our pace was now so slow we were barely moving ahead, step by step. My eyes refused to focus, my vision blurred, my dizziness increased. Sometimes I bent over with my hands hanging low in front of me to lighten my pack load, and some-times I stood straighter, with my head back and looking up into the trees. In this way I tried to vary the dense, gray fog of fatigue that was slowly enveloping me.

I began to doubt that we would ever make it to the *milpa*. The sun was out but the heavy canopy of trees hid it from sight. At about four kilometers Pablo dropped behind me and called out in a pitiful plea.

I stopped and shouted back to him in a hoarsely weak voice to get up and keep walking. He didn't answer. I stum-bled back and stood over him and repeated the command. He didn't move or answer. I fell to my knees and, shouting, shook him hard. He moaned and opened his eyes. He whispered something but I couldn't make it out. I managed to sit him up and gave him a drink of water from my canteen. He said he was finished and couldn't go another step.

My head was spinning and I was close to delirium. I lost my temper and in a rage I shouted that he was slowing us down. He was going to get us killed. He was weak, I finally said. Pablo told me to go ahead and leave him to die in peace. I began to shake him and try to drag him. I told him I wasn't leaving him to die and damn it, I'd drag him if I had to! My anger had given me some strength, and in a fit of rage and energy I hoisted him to his feet. He slumped to the ground and I, half out of my mind, began to drag him by one arm along the trail. He began to curse at me in Spanish.

I pulled him about ten feet before I had to drop him. I said if he didn't get on his feet, I'd drag him to the *milpa*. He got on his knees and tried to get up. He started to fall but I jerked him up by an arm. I could see he was ready to take a swing at me so I quickly stumbled back and started off down the trail. Pablo came on behind me, cursing and moaning.

The outburst relieved our tension and released what en-ergy we had left, and now our pace was a bit quicker. I knew there was still some fight left in the old boy, and in this mood of anger and determination we reached the six-kilometer point where I had placed the location of the *milpa*. I told Pablo we should see it any minute. After fifteen minutes we still hadn't, and Pablo was again whining steadily.

We struggled ahead another kilometer. Still no *milpa*. At one point, staggering and in a daze, I walked off the trail and fell into the jungle. Pablo walked right past me, slowly plodding on, his eyes on the ground. I got to my feet, pulling myself up by a small sapling, and followed him off down the trail. After awhile he realized I was not ahead of him and stopped. I called out and he turned around frightened. I passed by him and took the lead again.

Finally we came to my estimate of the eighth kilometer, and still no *milpa*. Pablo kept asking about it and I kept saying it was just ahead a little ways. Suddenly, before us, the jungle looked sunlit. Taking heart, I tried to step up my walk, but couldn't. Ahead I could see daylight through the trees.

"*La milpa!*" Pablo shouted, "*Gracias a Dios, la milpa!*" (Thank God, the cornfield!)

We reached the edge of the jungle and for the first time in weeks stepped out under the open sky. The *milpa* lay before us, drenched in sunlight! I broke out in a grin, but Pablo, haggard and glum, pushed by me and stumbled through the tangle of bushes and cornstalks ahead. It seemed an endless trek across it, but with the thought of the *ranchera* and food just ahead we weaved our unsteady way onward.

Finally we reached the far end of the *milpa* and without warning stepped out into a clearing. Above us on a rise stood the *ranchera*. Pablo made his way up the steep embankment and collapsed in front of it, motionless. I trudged in behind him and stood grinning in the sunlight at the old cornshed, which to us meant both salvation and civilization—but most of all, food.

It was stacked high with rows of corn and I must have stood there a full minute swaying, looking at it almost in disbelief, it seemed so unreal and beautiful. Then I checked my watch. It was just after two o'clock, and I realized that we had come twenty-two kilometers in seven hours—and with only two breaks! Incredible, in our condition, I thought, and as I looked up at the intense blue sky I suddenly went dizzy and felt weak all over. My legs gave way and I fell to the ground, rolled over on my pack and lost consciousness.

When I woke up, Pablo was already making the fire at the edge of the *ranchera*. I had only slept an hour but I felt rested enough to crawl over to the stacks of corn and begin degraining ear after ear. We soon had some water boiling in the coffee tin on the fire, and poured in several handfuls of corn. Pablo said it would take over an hour to soften them up to eat. I tossed some kernels of the pebble-hard corn in my mouth and tried to chew on them.

I stripped to the waist and sat up treating my tortured legs as best I could with some Listerine I had left, and letting my blanched, beaten body soak in the sun. My ribs showed clearly on my chest. I figured I must have lost twenty pounds. I had always been twenty pounds too light, and now, forty pounds underweight, it came to me that I looked like some of the pictures I remembered seeing of the prisoners at the concentration camps at the end of World War II. My arms were indented, bony and muscleless. But the world was beautiful! I lay back on the ground and enjoyed the heat of the sun and the comfort of being safe again, with food boiling on the fire.

I had started to doze off when I felt something on my leg. Lifting my head, I saw a foot-long green lizard perched on one of my thighs, staring at me. He was a little beauty. I sat up slowly but he jumped off and ran to the edge of the *ranchera* and stopped. I took a few of the grains of corn I had been chewing out of my mouth and threw them over to him, but he

wouldn't eat them. Later, while I sat there, taking notes, he
ran right across my legs again. Friendly little devil, I thought.

At four o'clock the corn was ready. It was an unbelievable
sensation to eat again. The corn was chewy but I couldn't remember when anything ever tasted better. My jaws were so
weak that in fifteen minutes they were aching and I had to rest
them. But on and off, we continued eating corn for two hours,
when, stuffed and feeling better, an overwhelming sleepiness
came over us. Wrapping ourselves in our hammocks, Pablo
and I stretched out on the ground near the fire, and throwing
Pablo's blanket over us we went to sleep.

5 · MULES BACK TO POPTÚN

THAT MORNING we were up at six A.M. My stomach ached. The
hard corn, plus the fact that I had overloaded it after eating
almost nothing for a week, had been too much. I felt nause-
ated and couldn't down another mouthful. Neither could
Pablo, so without eating we packed and left.

The trail to Concomá was open and clear, but we were not
out of the jungles yet, to recoin a phrase. We still had six kilometers to go to reach Concomá, and then another twenty to
Poptún.

My feet and legs were extremely painful, and I was limping badly. Pablo was not as bad, but he was sour and cranky.
He said if we could get two mules at Concomá, we might
make Poptún that afternoon; otherwise we would have to
spend a few days there resting and then walk in. I told him we
both needed penicillin and the sooner the better. We would
have to get mules at Concomá; if we didn't, I said, we might
both die from our infections.

My left leg was swollen badly and there was still the threat of gangrene. My system must have been half poisoned already. We hobbled along, at a slower pace than ever. After about four kilometers we heard voices up ahead and soon two men appeared. What a sight! The first human beings we had seen in over two weeks. It was Santiago of Concomá and a friend, going hunting.

We all smiled—Pablo for the first time in days. Santiago led us back the last two kilometers while his friend went off to hunt. We entered Concomá, straggling behind Santiago, and followed him into his house.

I lay in a hammock while some women made us something to eat. Pablo went out and came back wearing bright blue pants he had borrowed somewhere. Now he was smiling and happy. He had been worried about entering Poptún in his, which were filthy and torn to shreds. And in our condition, I thought; what vanity!

I lay in the hammock looking up at the thatched roof, thinking how strange and civilized it felt to be in a house again. Soon our food was ready. The women brought us a cup of corn soup (called *pozole*) and a small banana. Then we each ate five tortillas and two scrambled eggs, washing it all down with strong black coffee. Everything tasted great.

After we had eaten, Pablo told me that the people of Concomá did have two mules but let them roam freely through the jungle on days when they didn't use them. This was such a day. Santiago's brother Pedro had gone to see if he could round them up.

It was then after nine in the morning. By ten-thirty Pedro had not shown up and Santiago said that he probably would not find the mules until late in the afternoon, too late for us to start the long journey back to Poptún. Getting anxious and losing hope of getting back that day, I began to squeeze some of the festering spines out of my hands and legs.

We were happily surprised at eleven o'clock when Pedro showed up leading the two mules. He quickly readied them and I was offered the younger one, which had a saddle on it. The other mule, an old gray, was only cinched with a *pita* cover for a seat.

I no sooner had swung myself up into the saddle, when the mule gave two or three tremendous bucks and threw me off to the ground. I landed hard and the miserable animal proceeded to kick me several times in the arms and legs, until he was driven off. I was still so weak, and further dazed by the fall, that I didn't feel the pain of the kicks too badly. I simply got up and climbed on the other mule. This time I had better luck. The older animal was tame and friendly. I had no saddle, but at least I was still sitting on it.

Pablo got on the black mule, who didn't seem to mind him as much, and we waved our good-bys to Santiago and the other Kekchi Indians of Concomá. Pedro led my mule as we started out for Poptún.

I had never been on a mule before in my life, but I did pretty well. I didn't fall off once—and that without a saddle.

The trail, which led through ten kilometers of hilly, rocky country, was a river of mud. My mule kept going along the edge of it and slamming me into the trees. Pedro continually had to lead it straight again. We passed a coffee *finca* and I grabbed some of the green beans from the tree branches. They had a peculiar pasty taste.

After two hours of going through the rocky passes, under the tall green canopy of the jungle, at one o'clock we reached the flat plain of Poptún. There I took the reins.

The sun seemed warm and pleasant at first, but after three weeks of jungle shade it soon seemed as hot and dry as a burning desert. The plain was a flat expanse of brown grass, dotted here and there with an occasional pine tree or small *cerro*, and there was no shade on the trail. After an hour we were all wet with sweat, especially Pedro, who was walking ahead of us on the trail. We stopped once to take a break.

By now my backside was sore and aching. I put my hammock over the *pita* cover on the mule but it didn't seem to help much. The damage had been done, and soon every clumping step of the mule painful. The sun baked us in its bright heat, and the trail seemed endless. I rode along, in half-dazed dizziness, every part of my body aching. The mule ride had given it the final beating.

The trees back in the jungle, as the mule had thrown me against them, had whipped my leg sores open, and they were bleeding again. The end of my spine was at times almost too painful. I had imagined that after what I had been through nothing much could bother me any more, but my resistance was too low. I began to wonder if walking might have been easier. But I knew better. Neither Pablo nor I had any energy left and it was all I could do to stay mounted on my slowly plodding mule. The brief rest we had taken had proved that I could no longer really walk. I was now a hobbling half-cripple.

Finally the first few shacks on the outskirts of Poptún came into view. It took us another half hour to reach the edge of town. It reminded me of some unknown movie scene I had once seen.

We rode down the middle of the street, the mules slowly clomping along, as heads appeared out of doorways and windows. The people in the streets just stopped and stared. We must have looked more dead than alive. I could imagine their thoughts. Another crazy *gringo*, coming back from the jungle.

We pulled up in front of the hotel Sac-nite and, sliding off my mule, I found I could hardly stand up. I was weak and dizzy, my legs and feet ached and throbbed. Several people were standing around watching us, as were some children who had followed us through town.

Trying not to limp and look as badly beaten as I was, in

front of the crowd I paid Pedro six *quetzales* for his time and the mules and then gave Pablo seventy-five: sixty-three for his time in the jungle, at three *quetzales* a day, and twelve for the loss of his equipment in the capsize. I also gave him my hammock and canteen as *regalos*. I told him that as it was Friday and there was no plane out until Monday, I would see him in a day or two when we both felt better. He agreed and started for his house, with Pedro and the mules.

I watched them go down the road, and only then did I fully realize that the ordeal had ended, and with it my jungle adventure.

For all our hardships and our near encounters with death, I had come to find a new essence and meaning to life. The wild beauty of the jungle and the mood of the ruins of Machaquilá were things I would never forget. They had been worth the danger and the pain. Danger in itself is a thrilling experience, as long as one lives through it. And I had. I felt like a returning conqueror. But what had I returned to? Civilization . . . the glory of nine-to-five office hours, neurotics, pseudo-intellectuals, false morals, injustice, lies, TV and frozen foods. It was rather an empty feeling.

6 · BACK TO CIVILIZATION

I WENT INTO the hotel and ordered a room and a bath. The servants said nothing, staring at me wide-eyed as they went about their preparations. Looking in a mirror on the wall I could see why. Never had I seen such a bedraggled, beat-looking figure in my life.

The girl who showed me to my room said everyone thought we were dead. Now I understood the strange stares.

Carmen Acté had told them that we had gone on the cursed Machaquilá, and when we didn't show up after two weeks, they assumed the Rio had killed us. We were a week overdue, having spent exactly twenty-one days in the jungle.

Later, when I would tell how we had come back 148 kilometers without a machete, no one believed me. Impossible, they said, smiling. Without shoes and food yes, they argued, but not without a machete! To these people, to lose a machete in the jungle was considered sure death. Better to lose your right arm, one old man told me. Actually, they were calling me a liar in roundabout terms, but I had neither the strength nor inclination to argue with them. I knew and Pablo knew what we had been through and what we had accomplished; and besides, it was just good to be back and alive.

After dropping what gear I still had left in my room, I painfully hobbled out and bought a pack of Victor cigarettes. I smoked three in a row. Then I limped my way down to a dry-goods store and bought a pair of rubber shoes, a size too big. Cutting off the sandals, now rotten and covered with layers of mud, I barely got into them. I bought a new *pita* bag, soap, lighter fluid and some washwood. The last mentioned consists of fine strips of long, curled-up stringy pine wood, and is used instead of a washcloth for scrubbing the body.

Back at the hotel Sac-nite my bath was ready, an outside wooden stall with a bucket of hot water and a tub of cold water placed on the floor. A bit crude, but I never enjoyed a bath so much. Everything I did now seemed strangely new and better than ever. Little things that everyone takes for granted now were all luxuries to me. Eating, smoking, bathing, even sitting in a chair. One was given to me in the shower stall after I found I couldn't stand up and wash. Sitting in it, I spent a whole hour scrubbing my body with the tough piece of washwood.

When I had finished, Don Paco, the hotel owner, let me

borrow a pair of pants and a shirt while I had mine washed. I thought of going to the telegraph office to send a wire home, but my feet hurt too much. I would try the next day after a good meal and a night's rest.

Sitting on my bed, I began a ritual with needle and tweezers which was to go on for months. In the next few weeks along, I was to remove over a hundred spines from my feet and hands. Now that I was clean, most of them, and my leg wounds, were clearly visible.

I soon fell asleep to the sound of the late-afternoon rain beating on the tin roof, but was awakened an hour later for supper. A fabulous meal of rice, a meat-and-cabbage dish, an egg, spinach, tomato-and-onion omelette, bread, butter, jam and coffee. I ate so much I got dizzy. I was intoxicated with food.

For weeks to come, every hour I would get hungry. My appetite was insatiable. At seven I went out to buy some oranges and soon had finished three. Lying on my bed, I fell off to sleep again.

Later I woke up hungry. I hobbled out in the dim lit streets and came upon a bar. It was called *El Infierno* (Hell) and had badly done wall murals inside to prove the point. It was empty, except for the barmaid.

I ordered a fruit drink. She explained she had all kinds of liquor. I said, no, just a fruit drink, and proceeded to explain my condition. That led to a brief account of my jungle trip. She seemed very impressed and called in her girl friend from a back room.

The two were obviously prostitutes, the proverbial heart-of-gold type. They fussed over me and when I asked if there were any bananas I could buy in town said no. They were out of season. However, they said, they had sources, and produced a hand of nine large bananas, insisting I take it as a gift. After a half hour of talk in which I was invited to spend the night (I politely declined) I left. Getting between the sheets of my bed back at the hotel was a uniquely comfortable experience. I went out like a light.

At two in the morning I woke up to the sound of a heavy downpour on the roof. My feet ached so bad I spent two hours removing spines from them by the light of the kerosene lamp.

The next morning I was up at six. After a monumental breakfast with Don Paco, I hobbled off to the far end of town, a painful, limping kilometer, and sent a telegram to my parents. A classic of its type, it read:

ARRIVED SAFELY FROM JUNGLE. PLEASE SEND $150 TO MY ADDRESS IN QUEZALTENANGO. LOVE. YOUR SON AL

Nearby was the hospital, one of the larger buildings in town but still under construction. I went in but no doctors had arrived yet. I had to hobble back to the hotel and lie down for an hour, before I made the long trek back. When I arrived I waited for an hour with some people who were ahead of me in the clinic line. Finally I was called in.

The doctor had many questions to ask, mostly about how I had gotten in such a condition. He swabbed my legs with an antiseptic, cleaned out many of the wounds and applied a jellylike substance over them. Then he said that, prepared or unprepared, the *selva* was always dangerous. I said maybe just for *gringos*. He laughed and gave me a shot of penicillin. He told me to return that afternoon for another one and I agreed, but before I left I weighed myself on his scale. I had lost eighteen pounds on the old jungle trail, and was now down to 117.

Later, back at my hotel, Pablo came to visit me. He was smiling and in clean clothes, but it was obvious that he too had lost a lot of weight. We talked awhile, about how good it was to be alive, and before he left I gave him my frame pack as a *regalo.* I also told him to go to the hospital for a shot of penicillin and he agreed it would be best.

After lunch I slept awhile and later went down to the hospital myself for my second shot. There the doctor retreated my legs and this time bandaged them. He had no other patients after me and was in a talkative mood. We discussed my jungle trip, the States and Guatemala. His name was Fermin Baños Perez and he was a very pleasant sort of chap.

That night there was a local wedding being held in the movie theater. I limped down and found a hundred people standing outside, listening to the marimba music. A large door was open, and inside I could see the band up on the stage. Seven men playing two huge marimbas, a bass and a drum. They played very well and with gusto. On the floor of the theater at least 200 people were crammed together, dancing and whooping it up.

I stood there for awhile, talking to a man named Valério who had recognized me from my first few days at Poptún, and eating fried platanos from one of the stands. But the penicillin was taking effect. I was weak and my legs began to get heavy and ached.

I walked back to the hotel to the strains of the fading marimba, that old original Guatemalan instrument, wondering if the ancient Mayans had used it. I pictured it being played at a sacrificial rite and tried to reconcile its tones with the austerity of that atmosphere. I imagined that with the right composition it might add a strange grotesque, hypnotic spell to the mood of the event.

Back at the hotel I was asleep in minutes. A heavy rain woke me at two in the morning, and I lit the kerosene lamp and had a cigarette while I listened to its tropical downpour on the tin roof. My mood was one of lonely awareness. After awhile I got into bed and fell asleep to the staccato rhythm of the rain around me.

The following day I went to see Carmen Acté at his house
on the edge of town, a long painful walk on my aching legs.
We spent an hour talking of how Pablo and I had continued
on after he had left us. He was interested in all the cascades on
the Rio, and found it unbelievable that we had returned from
the ruin without machetes.

I said good-by to Carmen, thanking him for his part in my
adventure, and returned to the hotel. There I decided to settle
the bill with Don Paco, so as to figure what expenses I had
ahead. When the bill was paid I was left with eighteen *quetzales*. The plane fare to Guatemala City would be twelve, and
the bus to Quezaltenango three. That left me with another
three to play around with. A bit close for comfort.

I was still wearing Don Paco's clothes and went inside to
see if mine were ready. When I found they weren't the maid
said she would iron them dry *mañana*, so I did the job myself.
Then I squandered a dollar on a pair of socks. That night,
with nothing better to do, I had several games of dominoes
with Don Paco. I hadn't played in twenty years and he beat
me soundly every time.

The next day was Monday and the plane to Guatemala
City was due at ten in the morning. I was up early, had breakfast, packed and was ready to leave at nine. Awhile later Pablo
arrived. He had brought me a *regalo* of twenty Tusa cigarettes.
At ten we heard a plane overhead and started for the airport.
All that remained of my original 103 pounds of luggage was
my small *pita* shopping-type bag.

At the air strip I discovered that the plane that had landed
wasn't the Aviateca flight at all. It was a Guatemalan army
paratrooper plane, with cargo for the military base at Poptún.
I had already bought my ticket, but I asked to be put on it
anyway, as the regular plane would not arrive until one
o'clock. Luckily the captain of the aircraft said yes.

I turned to Pablo and we shook hands. I thanked him for

everything and we wished each other luck. It seemed a simple
farewell to the man who had been my constant companion for
three weeks in the jungle and who had risked his life with me.
We had had our arguments, true, but together we had saved
each other's lives, he at first and I in the final days. And together we had conquered a river and the jungle itself. Our 148-
kilometer (ninety-two mile) return trek from the ruins,
through dense jungle without a machete, will always remain
to me a vivid memory of my own stamina and courage—of
Pablo's—and of man's will to survive. What could I say to
Pablo except "*Gracias*"? I grasped his hand again, gave him
my poncho as a parting gift, and boarded the plane.

In a few minutes we were airborne and climbing steadily,
and soon Poptún had faded from view. The plane was empty
except for a row of iron seats along the walls, and two Guatemalan soldiers were up forward sleeping on them. I decided to
join them. After ten minutes the temperature dropped to
around sixty degrees and I shivered all the way to Guatemala
City, where we landed an hour later.

Hobbling across the field, as the plane had stopped far out
on a runway, I caught a cab to the first-class bus station in
town. The three-P.M. bus was full up and there would be nothing until the next morning. I had to leave that day as I had no
money left for a hotel room that night. After several inquiries
I managed to find a crosstown bus to the second-class station.

It was at a huge marketplace and literally dozens of buses
were all over the place, even among the stalls and Indians
selling their wares on the ground. Milling through the crowd
and asking dozens of drivers questions, as few of the buses had
signs of destination on them, I made my way along through
the utter confusion. Finally, and only by luck, I managed to
reach the right bus at twelve-thirty, just as it was leaving.

I jumped in front of it and it stopped. I got on while the
driver cursed and I paid him. I had to stand up the first hour,

but luckily someone got up right behind the driver and I jumped into the seat. Now I was ready for the 200-kilometer trip.

It was mostly uphill, a beautiful, winding but treacherous trail through the mountains. At times the overloaded old wreck of a bus crawled up the steep inclines, shifting, grinding and rumbling, and barely making it at a walking pace.

By four o'clock, when the first-class bus would already have been in Quezaltenango, we reached kilometer 130 and came to a rest stop. I had eaten three bananas on the way but I was starving. I had a tortilla meat sandwich and coffee, and once more we got on the old bus and crept on west, into the setting sun.

Shortly after six o'clock we entered *Xelajú* (Quezaltenango) and I went directly to the house of the Wiegands. They were surprised and happy to see that I had returned safely. A few letters were waiting for me, and a note from the bank. The money from my parents had beaten me there.

I spent the night talking with the Wiegands about my jungle trip, but they also had news for me. Hilda had gotten married. Later they got my old room ready and I went to bed early, tired from the day's travel.

I was up at dawn the next morning, going through the suitcase I had left there, and sorting out what I would take and what I would leave behind.

Shortly after six o'clock I heard what sounded like a heavy object crash down on the roof. Then the floor began to tremble. At first I didn't know what it was, but when I looked out and saw the cobblestones in the courtyard popping up and down, the realization hit me—earthquake!

The ground continued to tremble, harder and harder, and finally I went out and stood in the center of the courtyard. Eluvia, the Wiegand's maid, came running out of the kitchen in terror, shouting, *"Terremoto! terremoto!"* I calmed her down but when two large flowerpots shook off the wall and crashed into the courtyard she started in again. Then the tremor slackened off and stopped.

I wondered why the Wiegands hadn't gotten up, but didn't want to disturb them since it was all over. Later at breakfast they said they get two or three of these tremors a year, and they usually don't amount to much. Nobody had even bothered to get up.

That morning I went to the Banco Agricola Mercantil, off the Parque Centrale, and picked up my money. It took a dozen signatures. Next I picked up a few Christmas gifts in the local market, a beautiful rambling affair. Later I had a photo taken of myself in my jungle clothes at the Foto Estudio Portillo.

Before I left that night I slipped two dollars to Eluvia and told her not to mention it. She was extremely thankful and said I was a good man. I felt a pang of remorse. To the poor girl, what I had given her amounted to two weeks' pay.

The family came to the bus station with me at eight P.M. and saying good-by I thanked them for their hospitality and helpfulness. I slept all the way to Guatemala City. Again I went out for a midnight snack at the place off the parque, and returned to sleep in the bus.

I was at the airport early the next morning. With a stroke of luck, I found out there was an eight-A.M. plane leaving for Miami, instead of the scheduled one-o'clock flight. From there I would go to St. Petersburg, where my sister Rena and her husband Bob Sterns were living aboard their yawl *Sundance*. I wanted to see them and I also needed a few days' rest before getting back to New York. Also I needed more money to fly home, as I had decided that a bus trip of that length would have killed me in my condition.

As usual the plane was delayed. At ten o'clock our four-engine plane pulled up outside the terminal. We boarded and took off. I checked with the stewardess and discovered that our course would take us just west of Poptún and over the Rio Machaquilá.

Forty-five minutes later I spotted it! I looked down through the drifting clouds, with a deep, nostalgic feeling for that wild, unexplored Rio, and said a last farewell in silence. Somehow, it was sad.

GLOSSARY
of
Spanish, Mayan, and Other Terms Used in the Text

AGUA—Water
AGUANTA—Endure, bear, resist (hardships)
AMIGO—Friend
ARAÑA—A spider
ARMERIA—A gun shop
ARRADORES—Tiny red river bugs, cause itching, sores
ARROYO—A small stream, usually 5–25 feet wide, in El Petén, many dry up during the dry season of March and April
ARRÓZ—Rice
BEJUCOS—Vines
BANDIDO—Bandit, gangster
CAMBÓ—The heart of a sapling corozo palm, edible
CAMINO—Road, trail, way, passage
EL CAMINO ABIERTO—The open trail
CANTIMPLORA—Canteen (for holding liquids)

CASCADA—Waterfall (also, *cataráta, caída de água*)

CERRO—A hill

CHAMPA—A palm-branch lean-to

CHICLERO—A chicle-tree hunter: these men search out the chicle-gum tree, called *chico sapote*, deep in the Guatemalan jungles and tap it for its white sap, or chicle, from which chewing gum is made

COMIDA—A small informal restaurant: literally, food, supper

COROZÁL—A grove of corozo palm trees

DANTA—A small jungle deer: length, 4–5 feet

DE MI VIDA—Of my life

DIOS—God

ESPINA—Spine, thorn; also, splinter, fish bone

FAISANO—A pheasant

FINCA—Farm, ranch, plantation

FRIJOLES—Beans

FRONDS—The branches of a palm tree or fern, with the leaves attached directly to the stemlike branch

GALLO DE PELEAS—A fighting cock

GARAPATOS—Half-inch long gray ticks, very infectious

GLYPH—A Mayan carving, of a mostly undeciphered language

ÍDOLES—Idols (Guatemalans usually call the Mayan stelae by this name)

IGUANA—A tropical American lizard, grows to 5 feet or more in length

ISLA—Island

INDITA—A strong alcoholic drink, with an anise (licorice) flavor

JÚTES—Spiral-type snails, 2 inches long

KILOMETER—A unit of measure, of 1000 meters and equal to 3280 feet (there are 5 kms. in 3 miles, 8 in 5 miles and 40 in 25 miles; to convert kilometers into miles, divide them by eight and multiply by five)

LACANDONES—The last of the pure-blooded Mayans; 160 still live in the jungles of Chiapas, Mexico

LEGUA—A league (the Spanish league is 4 kilometers or 2½ miles, while the English league is 3 miles or 5 kms.)

LAGARTO—Alligator (actually, in Central America and South America there are only crocodiles; the only two species of alligators existing are in Florida and China)

LOCO—crazy, insane

MACHACA—A two-foot fish for which Rio Machaquilá is named; green, speckled white; humanlike teeth; eats nuts

MACHETE—The long swordlike knife, used in the tropics for cutting through the underbrush; blades vary between 17 and 24 inches in length

MAÍZ—Maize, corn

MANCOLOLA—A perdis bird, plum color, big as a hen

MAYAN—Ancient civilization of Guatemala and Mexico (A.D. 320–1697)

MECATE—25 square meters or about 240 square feet

METER—A unit of measure of slightly more than a yard, or 39.37 inches

MILPA—A cornfield (the ancient Mayan word for corn)

MIRA—Look, see

MONOS—Monkeys

MURCIÉLAGOS—Bats: the Guatemalan jungles abound with the bloodsucking vampire variety

NU-V BAR—An amazing food bar: weight, 1.5 ozs; lasts two years without refrigeration; each bar contains 200 calories, 8 grams protein, 8 of fat, 20 of carbohydrate, and ⅓ MDR of vitamins and minerals

PEMMICAN—A reddish-brown, pasty food, containing seedless raisins, peanuts, evaporated apples, dextrose, soy oil, hydrogenated shortening, vanilla extract and salt (some types also contain dried meat)

PACAIA—An edible, bitter-tasting flower shoot

PESO—Mexican currency: there are 12½ to a dollar; one peso is worth eight cents

PLAYA—A beach, the shore

POTSHERD—A broken piece of pottery, especially used to denote ancient ones

POZOLE—A soup made of fermented maize and water; when moldy, used to heal wounds (it has been analyzed and contains penicillin)

QUETZÁL—Guatemalan currency: one quetzal is equal to a dollar

QUINTÁL—100 pounds (pounds are called *libras* in Latin America)

RANCHERA—A small country house, a hut

RÁPIDO—A river rapid (also, *raudál*)

REGALO—A gift

RIO—River

RUINAS—Ruins

SANGRIAS—Bleed cuts, used to tap the chicle-gum tree

SARAGUÁTE—3-foot-tall monkey: dangerous if approached

SELVA—Literally, forest; in Latin America the jungle is always called *la selva*

STELA—An ancient Mayan monument, set upright in the ground and carved with figures and glyphs, varies from 5 to 10 feet high and 3 to 5 feet wide (plural: stelae)

TAPÍR—A gray, heavy-set 4-foot-long animal; resembles a pig but has a longer snout, resembling that of an ant-eater

TAPÓN—A blocked passage (landslide on road, tree across a river); literally: plug, stopper, bottle cap

TEQUILA—A strong, clear Mexican liquor, made from the maguey plant (before it is fully distilled, it is also drunk as a milky-white liquid, called *pulque*)

TERREMOTO—Earthquake

TIGRE—A tiger: in Latin America, all jungle cats are called tigers; in Central America there are three species—jaguar, puma and ocelot

TIRA—Shoot

TORCIDO—Cursed or ill-fated; literally, twisted

TORTILLAS—Ground corn, made into an unleavened pancake: the staple diet of Mexico and Guatemala, serving as bread

VÁMONOS—Let's go, we go (also, *vámos*)

VARA—One square meter

VIRGEN—Virgin

YUM KAAX—Name of ancient Mayan corn god

ZANCUDO—A large, long-legged mosquito with a half-inch stinger; can pierce leather

ZOCOLO—A public square or park, usually the main one of a town

ZOMPOPO—Leaf-cutting ants, a half inch or more in length; they have a stinging bite

ZOPILOTE—A vulture or buzzard; most of the tropical species have six-foot wingspans

CHART OF JUNGLE TRIP

DAY OF MONTH	DAY OF TRIP	KILOMETERS	EVENTS
NOV. 21	1	26	Left Poptún, passed Concomá, reached *milpa ranchera*.
22	2	8	Discovered cliff with caves. Explored it.
23	3	21	Shot *mancolóla* (a perdís bird)
24	4	8	Encounter with *saraguate*. Shot *faisano*. Reached Rio Machaquilá.
25	5	23	Carmen returned with mule. Pablo and I started down Rio. 7 tapons, 18 rapids.

DAY OF MONTH	DAY OF TRIP	KILOMETERS	EVENTS
26	6	17	21 rapids. Capsized in last. Lost one pack, both machetes, both our boots, etc. 4 cascades.
27	7	5	Came upon 11 cascades.
28	8	6	15 cascades.
29	9	9	14 cascades.
30	10	13	Took puncture in boat. 4 cascades, 11 rapids, 2 tapons, caught *machaca* fish.
DEC. 1	11	Rio 7 Land 12	8 cascades. Arrived at ruins of Machaquilá. Brief exploration.
2	12	12	Explored ruin, started back.
3	13	8	Swamp. Pablo almost left me.
4	14	12	Reached Dos Arroyos.
5	15	12	Shot off last pistol round.
6	16	16	Smoked last cigarette. Passed La Cuchara. Reached El Presidente.
7	17	12	Became lost in the jungle.
8	18	12	No food left. Reached La Machaca.
9	19	16	Reached open trail.
10	20	22	Exhaustion, hunger. Reached *milpa*.
11	21	26	Reached Concomá, then Poptún by mules.

A Brief Chronology of
Mayan Civilization

(Dates are based on the Goodman-Hernández-Thompson correlation. Herbert J. Spinden's system of dating, places the dates 260 years earlier.)

B.C. Oct. 14, 3373. According to Spinden this is the "zero date," from which all Mayan calendrical readings were made.

B.C. 3113. Mayan "zero date" used by Goodman-Hernández-Thompson.

B.C. 2000. Probable date, when Mayas changed from nomadic hunters, to sedentary farmers.

A.D. 320. Leyden Plate: earliest dated object so far discovered.

328 Stela 9, Uaxactún: earliest dated monument.

300–900 Classic Old Empire: Centered in El Petén. All achievements brought to their zeniths. Machaquilá flourished, 741–815.

889 Date of last three stelae from Classic period (At Uaxactún, Xultún, and Xamantún).

987 In Yucatán, Mayapán is settled by the Itzás, a warrior people from the Mexican plateau.

1441 The destruction of Mayapán by the Xius, the powerful ruling family of Uxmal, ends centralized authority.

1464–1515 Hurricane, pestilence, wars and plague, devastate Mayan society.

1502 Christopher Columbus is first white man to see the Maya.

March 3, 1517. Hernández de Córdoba, lands, and makes first contact with Mayas, in Yucatán.

1546 In Yucatán, the slaughter and conquest of the Maya, by the Spanish.

March 13, 1697. Last Mayan city conquered. Tayasál, on lake Petén-Itzá, falls to Martin de Ursua.

1958 Pablo Paredes discovers ruins of Machaquilá.

Dec. 24, 2011. Mayan prediction of final annihilation of civilization on Earth.

BIBLIOGRAPHY

BLOM, FRANS, and OLIVER LA FARGE.
  Tribes and Temples. Two volumes. New Orleans, 1926.
BRAINERD, GEORGE W.
  The Maya Civilization. Southwest Museum. Los Angeles. 1954.
COVARRUBIAS, MIGUEL
  The Eagle, the Jaguar, and the Serpent: Indian Art of the Americas. Knopf. New York. 1954.
COE, MICHAEL D.
  The Maya. Praeger. New York. 1966.
GALLENKAMP, CHARLES
  Maya. Pyramid, Worlds of Science edition. New York. 1962.
LANDA, DIEGO de
  Relación de las cosas de Yucatán. Merida. 1938.
MALER, TEOBERT
  Researches in the Central Portion of the Usumatsintla Valley.

Cambridge, Mass., Peabody Museum of American Archaeology and Ethnology, Harvard University, "Memoirs," Vol. II, 1901–1903.

MORLEY, SYLVANUS G.
The Ancient Maya. 3rd edition, rev. by George W. Brainerd. Stanford University Press. Stanford, California. 1956.

PROSKOURIAKOFF, TATIANA
An Album of Maya Architecture. University of Oklahoma Press. 1963.

SPINDEN, HERBERT J.
"In Quest of Ruined Cities." *Scientific American.* Vol. 138, No. 2. (1928).

STEPHENS, JOHN L.
Incidents of Travel in Central America, Chiapas and Yucatán. Two volumes. New York. 1841.

THOMPSON, J. ERIC S.
The Rise and Fall of Maya Civilization. University of Oklahoma Press. Norman, Oklahoma. 1954.

VON HAGEN, VICTOR W.
World of the Maya. Mentor. New York. 1960.

WAUCHOPE, ROBERT
They Found the Buried Cities. University of Chicago Press. Chicago. 1965.

INDEX